WAKING FROM THE FOG

SUPPORTING SURVIVORS OF NARCISSISTIC ABUSE

J. PRATAP

Made with ♥ on the Notion Press Platform
www.notionpress.com

Contents

Foreword

Narcissistic abuse is insidious, leaving victims in a state of confusion, self-doubt, and emotional exhaustion. It's a journey that can feel isolating, with the fog of manipulation clouding your sense of reality. Waking from the Fog was written to help you break free from that fog and begin the healing process—whether you're recovering from abuse or supporting someone who is.

This book blends practical strategies with spiritual wisdom, offering a roadmap to understanding narcissistic behavior, reclaiming your sense of self, and rebuilding a life rooted in self-worth and empowerment. Through the teachings of the Bhagavad Gita and real-world advice, I aim to provide you with the tools to heal, grow, and regain the peace you deserve.

Healing from narcissistic abuse is not easy, and it's not linear. But with patience, reflection, and the right support, you can move beyond the pain and find the clarity and strength to move forward. This book is your guide to waking up from the fog and stepping into a future of freedom, joy, and self-love.

You are not alone, and you are worth the journey.

— J. Pratap

Preface

"The strongest people are those who win battles we know
nothing about."

In our lives, we often encounter toxic individuals. They can be found in our families, friendships, workplaces, and even in places we trust, like temples or community centers. Understanding the impact of psychological abuse is essential for healing and moving forward.

The Hidden Struggles of Psychological Abuse

Psychological abuse can be sneaky. It often leaves no visible scars, but it deeply affects how we feel about ourselves. Imagine riding an emotional rollercoaster: one moment you're on top of the world, and the next, you're plummeting into despair. This can happen in relationships where someone constantly undermines you or in a job where your boss belittles your efforts.

You might feel overwhelmed and confused, even questioning your own worth. It's common to feel guilty for standing up for yourself against someone who treats you poorly. You're not alone in these feelings, and recognizing them is the first step toward healing.

Emotional Abuse vs. Psychological Abuse

Many people confuse emotional abuse with psychological abuse. While both can harm individuals, they differ in intent and impact. Emotional abuse often comes from people who struggle with their own issues, like addiction. For instance, a loved one may lash out when under the influence but can apologize once they seek help.

On the other hand, psychological abuse is deliberate. It involves individuals who hurt others for the sake of power and control. Picture a manipulative partner who enjoys seeing you upset or a boss who belittles their employees to feel superior. These abusers often play mind games, finding satisfaction in your discomfort. Their enjoyment may not be obvious, but you can often sense it in their behavior.

Recognizing Hidden Abuse

Psychological abuse is often referred to as "hidden abuse" because it can be subtle and difficult to identify at first. Just like you can't see toxins in water until it starts harming you, the effects of this abuse can go unnoticed until they become severe. Initially, the actions of an abuser might be so slight that you dismiss them. But over time, they may become more apparent, leaving you feeling confused and doubting yourself.

Many who seek counseling often think they must change to stop the abuse. They believe that if they become stronger, the situation will improve. However, psychological abusers thrive on the idea that their victims will change while they remain unchanged. Victims often fall into the trap of self-blame, thinking they must be the problem. This cycle can feel overwhelming, but part of healing is uncovering the truth and separating it from the lies told by the abuser.

The Importance of Education

As you start to recognize these patterns, it's essential to understand that psychological abuse and emotional abuse are different. The more you know, the more empowered you become. For example, imagine a workplace where a boss constantly criticizes their employees. This behavior is psychological abuse, aimed at maintaining control and superiority.

In your healing journey, you'll learn to recognize common abusive behaviors. This knowledge is powerful because it helps you understand that you're not "crazy." Abusers often share similar traits, making their actions predictable.

Let's say you begin to notice that your friend always makes you feel inadequate during conversations. Recognizing this pattern allows you to set boundaries and protect your self-esteem.

Finding Clarity and Support

Some readers may be far along in their recovery journey, while others may just be starting or feeling lost. No matter where you are, remember that with time and support, clarity and healing are possible. Recognizing that you've been in an abusive relationship is a gradual process, especially since the damage is often hidden within.

Understanding how abusers operate can lift the weight of confusion off your shoulders. Knowing the signs of abuse can help you avoid toxic individuals in the future. Many survivors start feeling lost, but education can help you spot red flags early.

A Key Realization

People often wonder how they ended up in an abusive relationship. A critical realization is that abusers target specific individuals and know exactly what they're doing. They use lies and manipulation. Acknowledging this is crucial for healing. It's easy to feel pity for abusers, but this mindset can trap you in a cycle of excuses and prevent recovery.

Empaths—people who are highly sensitive and compassionate—often fall victim to these abusers. They exploit the tenderness of empaths, making education essential for breaking this cycle.

Moving Forward

As you continue through this chapter, take your time to reflect on the material. Use a Personal Reflections journal to actively engage with the content. This approach will help you build strength and confidence, making you less likely to fall prey to future abusers.

Whether or not you've experienced an abusive relationship, this chapter will provide you with a deeper understanding of psychological abuse. By increasing awareness and knowledge about this issue, we can help bring it into the open and reduce its impact on people's lives.

Remember, the journey to healing is not just about surviving but thriving. Embrace your strength, and know that you have the power to create a healthier and happier future.

Acknowledgements

Writing this book has been a deeply personal and transformative journey, and it would not have been possible without the support of many individuals. First and foremost, I want to express my heartfelt gratitude to the brave survivors of narcissistic abuse who shared their stories, struggles, and triumphs. Your courage, resilience, and willingness to heal continue to inspire me.

I am deeply grateful to the mentors, therapists, and spiritual guides who have shaped my understanding of narcissistic abuse and the healing process. Your wisdom, guidance, and compassion have been invaluable in helping me write this book.

Finally, to you, the reader—whether you are healing from narcissistic abuse or helping someone else on their journey—thank you for trusting me to be part of your path. I hope the insights shared in this book serve as a guide, offering you the tools and support you need to reclaim your life and well-being.

This book is dedicated to all of you.

— J. Pratap

Prologue

Many of us start as happy and kind individuals, eager to spread positivity. After facing challenges and disappointments, it's easy to feel overwhelmed by negativity. However, it's our responsibility to maintain that joy and kindness within ourselves. By choosing to embrace compassion instead of contempt, we can reclaim our happiness and prevent our experiences from defining who we are. If we can maintain kindness toward those who have hurt us, it shows true strength and resilience—perhaps indicating that we are becoming better people in the process. Focusing on kindness not only aids our own healing but also creates a ripple effect of positivity in the world around us.

Transforming pain into wisdom is a journey of resilience; each challenge faced becomes a lesson learned, shaping our understanding of ourselves and the world. Through acceptance, we no longer allow our past to define us, but instead, we embrace it as a vital part of our growth, paving the way for a future filled with strength, compassion, and hope.

CHAPTER ONE

WHY YOU?

"Those who feel threatened often seek to diminish the light they cannot bear to shine beside."

Abusers often have a keen eye for the strengths and qualities in others that they lack. This can manifest in various settings—workplaces, friendships, or even within families. For instance, a narcissistic coworker may target a talented colleague simply out of envy for their achievements. Initially, these abusers may admire the qualities that make their target successful, but once they gain control, their focus shifts. They aim to undermine those very traits, belittling the person's intelligence or confidence to assert their own superiority.

It's vital for survivors of such abuse to recognize that being targeted does not equate to weakness. Consider a sociopath who insults someone's appearance or social standing, even though those traits initially drew them in. This cycle of jealousy drives them to dismantle the qualities they once admired, leaving their victim feeling confused and diminished.

Imagine relationships with these abusers as a strategic game of chess. A manipulative partner may isolate their victim from friends and family, moving pieces on the board to serve their own interests. The abuser's sole focus is control, often disregarding the emotional toll their actions take on the survivor.

For survivors, understanding that abusers do not have their best interests at heart is crucial. Instead of becoming trapped in the abuser's manipulative schemes, the path to recovery lies in building a fulfilling, healthy life. Educating oneself about narcissism, sociopathy, and psychopathy can be empowering. While some may view narcissism as a common human flaw, others sensationalize these traits in movies and television, obscuring the reality of the harm they cause.

A common misconception is that personality disorders are akin to mental health issues such as bipolar disorder or depression. In truth, personality disorders often stem from unhealthy childhood relationships. For example, a child who is excessively pampered might grow up believing they are above the rules, leading them to exploit others throughout their life. Conversely, some individuals who experience emotional neglect might develop less empathy; however, that does not excuse abusive behavior.

Many who face difficult childhoods emerge as compassionate adults, striving to improve themselves. In stark contrast, narcissists and sociopaths typically refuse to acknowledge their issues. They perceive their actions as justified and shy away from meaningful self-reflection or therapy. Their harmful behavior persists because it serves their interests. While everyone may act selfishly at times, most people feel regret and seek to make amends. Narcissists, on the other hand, consistently blame others and view themselves as flawless.

For survivors, the journey to healing begins with understanding that they are not to blame for the abuse they endured. Embracing personal strengths and cultivating supportive connections can help reclaim their lives and foster resilience. Remember, it's not about weakness; it's about harnessing the strength to rise above adversity and create a brighter future.

Recognizing the dynamics of abuse is the first step toward healing. By understanding the motivations of abusers and the impact of their behavior, survivors can begin to reclaim their power. Building a supportive network, prioritizing self-care, and educating oneself about these patterns are essential in moving forward. Healing is a journey, and each step taken toward understanding and self-empowerment is a step closer to a life filled with joy and authenticity.

Narcissistic abuse can be one of the most confusing and emotionally damaging experiences a person can endure. The psychological toll of being manipulated, belittled, and controlled by someone who once seemed to admire you is difficult to process. If you've found yourself caught in the web of a narcissist's emotional and psychological manipulation, it's natural to ask: Why does this happen? Why do narcissists treat others this way? What motivates them to hurt those they claim to care about?

Understanding why narcissists abuse others is crucial to freeing yourself from their toxic grip. Narcissistic abuse is not about your worth or weakness; it is rooted in the narcissist's deep-seated insecurities, fragile self-esteem, and overwhelming need for control and validation. In this chapter, we will explore the psychological and emotional reasons why narcissists abuse people, how their behaviors are rooted in their own dysfunction, and how you can start to recognize and heal from the damage they cause.

1. Narcissists Abuse to Feel Superior

At the heart of narcissistic abuse is an overwhelming need for superiority. Narcissists feel that the world revolves around them and believe they are more important, talented, or deserving than others. This need for dominance is driven by a fragile sense of self-esteem and a fear of being exposed as ordinary or unremarkable.

Narcissists often seek out people who have qualities they lack, whether it's beauty, intelligence, success, or confidence. In the early stages of a relationship, they may shower their targets with praise, admiration, and affection because these traits reflect the very qualities the narcissist wishes they had. This initial admiration, often referred to as "love bombing," can make you feel special and appreciated. But once the narcissist begins to feel threatened by your strengths or accomplishments, their admiration quickly turns into resentment and envy.

Why does this happen? The narcissist sees your talents and success as a reflection of their own inadequacy. In their eyes, someone else's brilliance makes their own worth seem diminished. Rather than celebrate your achievements or share in your success, they seek to tear you down in an attempt to restore their own sense of superiority. They will belittle your accomplishments, criticize your choices, and try to make you feel inferior—all in an effort to keep their own fragile ego intact.

This dynamic often leads to gaslighting: the narcissist manipulates you into doubting your own reality, making you second-guess your experiences. If they once praised your intelligence and now insult it, you might wonder if you've changed or if you are misremembering their previous admiration. This cycle of admiration followed by devaluation is a hallmark of narcissistic abuse, leaving victims feeling emotionally confused and uncertain.

2. Narcissists Abuse to Maintain Control

Another key reason narcissists abuse others is their obsession with control. Narcissists view relationships as power struggles. Whether in a romantic partnership, a friendship, or a work relationship, their primary goal is to dominate the other person and assert their control over them. This need for control often manifests as manipulation and emotional abuse, and it is not limited to any one type of relationship.

Narcissists begin their manipulation by slowly gaining your trust and admiration. They will use tactics like flattery, charm, and even promises of love or loyalty. But once they feel they have secured their position and gained your emotional dependence, they begin to manipulate the situation to their advantage. They may use guilt-tripping, emotional blackmail, or isolation tactics to ensure that you are cut off from other sources of support.

A narcissist may subtly isolate you from friends, family, or colleagues, convincing you that you don't need them, that they are the only one who truly understands or cares about you. This tactic makes you more dependent on them, increasing their control over your emotional and mental state. Narcissists are skilled at creating confusion in their relationships, using tactics like gaslighting, where they deny or distort the truth to make you question your own perceptions and emotions. They want to make you feel disoriented, so you will rely on them for clarity and direction.

The narcissist's obsession with control is rooted in their fear of vulnerability. If they can control your every move, your thoughts, and your feelings, they believe they can protect themselves from being exposed as imperfect. By manipulating and controlling you, they are able to maintain the false image of perfection that they desperately cling to. Your independence and self-confidence are perceived as threats to this control, which is why they actively try to undermine and suppress them.

3. Narcissists Abuse Because of Their Fragile Self-Esteem

A common misconception about narcissists is that they are supremely confident and have unshakable self-esteem. In reality, narcissists often have a fragile self-image that they cover up with grandiosity and arrogance. Their exaggerated sense of self-importance is a defense mechanism designed to protect them from feelings of inadequacy and self-doubt.

Narcissists thrive on external validation. They need constant praise, admiration, and attention to feel good about themselves. Their self-worth is entirely dependent on how others perceive them. As a result, they will target people who possess qualities they lack and use them to bolster their own sense of self-importance.

When the narcissist sees someone with greater success, confidence, or talent, they feel threatened. They may begin by trying to manipulate and control that person to prevent them from surpassing the narcissist in any way. As the relationship progresses, the narcissist will work to diminish those very qualities they once admired. They might insult your intelligence, belittle your achievements, or criticize your appearance—anything to make you feel small and unworthy.

This is not a reflection of you, but of their insecurities. Narcissists cannot tolerate anyone else being in the spotlight because it threatens their fragile sense of self. By reducing you to something "lesser," they temporarily feel better about themselves. This cycle of admiration followed by devaluation is the narcissist's way of keeping their self-esteem intact, even though it's built on a shaky foundation.

4. Narcissists Abuse Because They Lack Empathy

One of the most damaging traits of narcissists is their lack of empathy. Narcissists are often unable—or unwilling—to understand or care about the feelings of others. This lack of emotional depth means that they can harm people without feeling guilty, remorseful, or concerned about the impact of their actions. Instead, they view others as tools to serve their own needs, rather than as individuals with their own emotions and desires.

When a narcissist emotionally abuses someone, they are often unaware or indifferent to the pain they cause. They may lash out, insult, or humiliate their target without a second thought, as they simply don't understand what they are doing to you. Their only concern is how the situation impacts them. If you challenge them, point out their behavior, or try to set boundaries, they will dismiss your feelings, accusing you of being overly sensitive or unreasonable.

The narcissist's lack of empathy is not an accident—it is a result of their self-centered worldview. They believe that their needs, desires, and feelings are the only ones that matter. This is why they cannot acknowledge the hurt they cause, and why they often blame others for any problems in the relationship. To the narcissist, they are always the victim, and you are always the cause of their pain. This emotional cruelty is the hallmark of narcissistic abuse.

5. Narcissists Abuse to Reinforce Their False Sense of Identity

Narcissists often construct a false sense of self—an inflated persona that is designed to protect them from their own feelings of inadequacy. This false self is built on grandiosity, superiority, and a desire for admiration. It is a defensive shield that they use to protect themselves from the vulnerabilities they refuse to acknowledge.

When this false self is threatened—by your success, your independence, or your ability to challenge them—the narcissist will do whatever it takes to preserve it. This may include attacking your character, spreading lies, or making you doubt your own worth. They are so invested in maintaining their perfect image that they will often destroy others in the process.

Narcissists need to see themselves as flawless, and they are deeply uncomfortable with any suggestion that they might be wrong or flawed. When their image is threatened, they will react with rage, defensiveness, or cruel behavior, all in an attempt to protect the illusion of their perfection. They cannot tolerate being exposed as vulnerable or imperfect, so they shift the focus onto you, turning the tables and blaming you for the problems in the relationship.

6. Narcissists Abuse Because They Enjoy the Power

Lastly, many narcissists engage in abusive behavior because they derive pleasure from the power and control they have over others. Narcissists thrive on attention and admiration, but they also enjoy the dominance they hold over their victims. Seeing someone suffer, struggle, or feel diminished gives the narcissist a sense of control and superiority. This sadistic pleasure is an added motivation for their abusive behavior.

The more they can manipulate, belittle, and confuse you, the more they feel energized and empowered. The narcissist feeds off the emotional chaos they create, using it to fuel their ego and maintain a sense of importance. This hunger for power is not just about feeling good—it's about feeling better than everyone else, especially those who dare to challenge them or have the qualities.

HOW YOU'RE DRAWN IN

"Beware the smile that masks a storm; true connections uplift, while manipulation seeks to control."

Imagine a skilled actor stepping onto a stage, mastering the art of manipulation with such precision that every move, every word, feels perfectly timed and believable. Now, think of psychological abusers as equally skilled performers, but instead of captivating an audience for applause, they use their charm and calculated tactics to control and harm those around them. Their performances are designed to deceive, twist reality, and ultimately break you down, all while keeping you wondering whether the problem is truly them—or if it's somehow you.

In this chapter, we will explore how you can become entangled in the web of narcissistic abuse. How does someone, often kind, strong, and independent, find themselves in such a toxic, emotionally draining relationship? The answer lies in the manipulative strategies that narcissists use to draw you in, and the subtle ways they chip away at your sense of self. In the beginning, spotting the warning signs of abuse can be nearly impossible, as the manipulative tactics are cleverly concealed beneath a veil of charm, affection, and false promises.

The Illusion of Perfection: How It Begins

At first, everything seems perfect. The narcissist is everything you've ever wanted in a partner, friend, or colleague. They are charismatic, attentive, and flattering, making you feel like the most important person in the world. They might shower you with affection, praise, and gifts, pulling you into their orbit. It's easy to see how someone could fall for this attention, especially if you're feeling lonely or vulnerable. In these moments, it can feel like a dream come true, as if you've finally met someone who sees and appreciates you for exactly who you are.

However, just as quickly as the narcissist appears to shower you with affection, they begin to subtly test your boundaries, poking at your vulnerabilities, and subtly shifting the relationship dynamic. The early signs of manipulation are hidden behind a cloak of charm, making it hard to identify the threat. They may listen intently to your deepest insecurities or your most intimate stories, only to later use that information against you.

These early manipulations are often hard to detect because they don't come with big red flags. Instead, the narcissist relies on small, calculated moves that may seem inconspicuous at first but eventually add up to a deep emotional and psychological toll. A cutting comment here, a dismissive glance there, and before you know it, your once-strong sense of self begins to erode.

The Tactics They Use: Psychological Chess

Narcissists are not simply acting out of random impulse; they have honed their tactics over time. Think of their behavior as a psychological chess game, with each move designed to maintain their dominance and control. Their goal is not only to manipulate but also to undermine your sense of reality, making you feel as though you're always the one at fault, or that you're "overreacting" to their harmful actions. This ongoing confusion can leave you second-guessing your own instincts, unsure of whether the problem lies with you or them.

One of the most common tactics they employ is gaslighting. This term refers to the narcissist's ability to manipulate you into questioning your own perception of reality. They may twist facts, deny conversations or events, or simply insist that you're misremembering things. For example, a narcissist might say, "I never said that," or "You're being too sensitive," even when you have clear evidence to the contrary. Over time, this gaslighting causes you to doubt your own memory, feelings, and sense of self-worth.

Another tactic is projection, where the narcissist projects their flaws and insecurities onto you. They may accuse you of things they themselves are guilty of—lying, cheating, being selfish—while deflecting blame from their own actions. This leaves you in a constant state of self-doubt and confusion, always wondering whether you're truly in the wrong or whether they're simply shifting the blame to avoid taking responsibility.

Emotional Manipulation: The Subtle Weaving of Control

Emotional manipulation is perhaps the most insidious weapon in the narcissist's arsenal. They exploit your emotions, making you feel guilty, inadequate, or unworthy for things that are not your fault. This form of control often comes in the guise of love, where the narcissist convinces you that they are the only one who can truly understand and care for you. However, their affection is conditional—given only when you meet their needs or fulfill their desires.

One of the primary ways narcissists exert control is through guilt-tripping. They may manipulate you into feeling responsible for their emotions, turning the tables so that you feel guilty for their unhappiness. For example, if you disagree with them or set boundaries, they might say, "I can't believe you're treating me like this after everything I've done for you," or "If you really loved me, you would never do that." This makes you feel as though you are the one causing the harm, when in reality, they are manipulating you into submission.

Additionally, narcissists are often experts at emotional withholding. They may withhold affection, love, or attention when you fail to comply with their wishes, creating an environment where you constantly strive for approval and validation. This behavior can lead to a trauma bond, where you become emotionally addicted to their intermittent affection, making it even harder to break free from the cycle of abuse.

The Weight of Small Hurts: How Abuse Accumulates

In the early stages of a narcissistic relationship, it's easy to brush off hurtful comments or subtle manipulations. But over time, these small hurts begin to accumulate, like pebbles piling up in a bag. At first, each pebble may feel insignificant, but as more are added, the weight becomes unbearable. You might begin to feel emotionally drained, constantly walking on eggshells, uncertain of what will trigger the narcissist's next outburst or manipulation.

Each small instance of criticism, emotional neglect, or gaslighting feels like a drop in the bucket. But eventually, that bucket becomes too heavy to carry. The accumulation of these emotional cuts can leave you feeling exhausted, defeated, and disconnected from your own sense of identity.

Recognizing the small hurts is an essential part of breaking free from narcissistic abuse. You might wonder why something that seemed minor at the time still hurts so much. The truth is that these repeated offenses erode your sense of self-worth, leaving you questioning your value and ability to trust your own perceptions.

Recognizing the Signs of Psychological Abuse

If you find yourself in a situation where emotional confusion, self-doubt, and anxiety are your daily reality, it's time to take a step back and reflect. Recognizing the signs of narcissistic abuse can be the first step toward reclaiming your sense of self. Here are a few warning signs that may indicate you're in an abusive relationship:

Constant Criticism: If the person in your life frequently undermines your confidence, dismisses your opinions, or makes you feel less than you are, it's a major red flag.

Gaslighting: If you find yourself questioning your memory or feeling like you're "losing touch with reality," it's time to pay attention. Narcissists are experts at distorting the truth to serve their own narrative.

Isolation: Narcissists often try to isolate you from friends and family to maintain control. If you notice your social circle shrinking or that your relationships with others are being sabotaged, it's an intentional manipulation tactic.

Love Bombing: The narcissist may initially overwhelm you with affection, compliments, and promises of forever. This idealization phase is designed to hook you in, making it difficult to see their true nature until much later.

Inconsistent Behavior: Narcissists often exhibit erratic behavior—being sweet one moment and cruel the next. This inconsistency creates emotional whiplash, making you feel emotionally unstable and constantly seeking their approval.

The Power of Self-Reflection

Breaking free from the cycle of abuse requires deep introspection. It's important to ask yourself the tough questions:

How do I feel when I'm around this person? If you constantly feel anxious, insecure, or second-guessing yourself, it may be a sign that the relationship is toxic.

Do I often feel like I'm walking on eggshells? If you're always worried about setting the person off, it's an indication that their behavior is emotionally manipulative.

Am I made to feel guilty for expressing my needs or desires? Narcissists thrive on silencing others and dismissing their needs in favor of their own.

Self-reflection helps you recognize the patterns of abuse and understand the emotional toll it's taking on you. Acknowledging that you've been manipulated is the first step toward reclaiming your life and setting boundaries that protect your emotional well-being.

Seeking Support: You Don't Have to Do This Alone

It's easy to feel isolated when you're in a relationship with a narcissist, as they often work to separate you from your support network. However, seeking help and talking to trusted friends, family members, or a therapist can provide the validation and perspective you need to see the situation for what it is. Sharing your experiences with others can open your eyes to the patterns of abuse you may have overlooked or normalized.

Support groups can also be incredibly helpful, as they provide a safe space where you can hear stories from others who have gone through similar experiences. Realizing that you are not alone can empower you to take the necessary steps to protect yourself and begin the healing process.

CHAPTER THREE

HOW IT SHAPES YOU

"The trials we face shape our spirit, turning wounds into wisdom and pain into power."

In our journey to understand psychological abuse, we've explored its roots and the intricate tactics narcissists use to manipulate their victims. However, the effects of narcissistic abuse run much deeper than the manipulation itself. They ripple out and begin to reshape the very core of who a person is, transforming someone once strong, confident, and emotionally healthy into someone struggling with self-doubt, insecurity, and confusion. This chapter is about that transformation—how narcissistic abuse can alter your personality and the long-lasting impact it can have on your sense of self.

Survivors of narcissistic abuse often begin their relationships with a strong foundation of emotional resilience, adaptability, and hopefulness. These are the very qualities that initially attract the narcissist, who sees them as opportunities to exploit. But as the relationship deepens and the abuse escalates, these same qualities—resilience, empathy, self-confidence—become vulnerabilities, gradually chipping away at the survivor's identity. It's heartbreaking to witness someone who once radiated positivity and confidence being reduced to a shell of their former self, consumed by self-doubt and insecurity.

Understanding how narcissistic abuse shapes you requires us to take a closer look at the internal shifts that occur in a survivor's psyche. Narcissistic abuse doesn't just leave visible scars; it rewires your thinking, emotions, and behaviors, often leaving you questioning your own worth and sanity. This is not a result of your personal shortcomings; it's a byproduct of the prolonged manipulation and emotional torture you have endured.

The Shift in Self-Perception

Many survivors of narcissistic abuse were once self-assured individuals, confident in their decisions, clear about their values, and secure in their sense of self. They had a solid understanding of who they were and what they wanted from life. But over time, the repeated emotional blows delivered by a narcissistic partner—whether through gaslighting, devaluation, or emotional withdrawal—gradually undermined their self-esteem and sense of reality.

Before the abuse began, the survivor may have been someone who felt strong, valued, and in control of their own life. After months or even years of being manipulated, dismissed, or outright devalued by the narcissist, however, this person may start to question every decision they make. They may begin to feel as though nothing they do is ever good enough. They may even feel like they don't deserve better, or that they're unworthy of love and respect. This shift in self-perception is one of the most profound and painful consequences of narcissistic abuse.

One of the key reasons narcissistic abuse has such a profound effect on a survivor's personality is because narcissists are experts at using manipulation and emotional blackmail to alter how their victims view themselves. By constantly devaluing their victim's thoughts, emotions, and achievements, they create an environment where the survivor becomes increasingly unsure of their own abilities. This can lead to feelings of inadequacy, anxiety, and emotional numbness, which can alter how the survivor interacts with others and even how they perceive their own worth.

Codependency vs. Empathy: The Confusion of Selfless Love

A major misunderstanding about survivors of narcissistic abuse is that they are often seen as needy, overly dependent, or unable to function without others.

In reality, many survivors were emotionally strong, independent, and secure before entering into a relationship with a narcissist. What happens over time, though, is that the abuse gradually chips away at their self-reliance and forces them into a cycle of codependency. But it's important to differentiate between codependency and being an empath, which is a common trait of narcissistic abuse victims.

Codependency involves an unhealthy entanglement, where one person enables another's dysfunction, making it harder for both parties to grow. Codependent individuals feel as though their worth is tied to the approval or well-being of others. In abusive relationships, this manifests as the survivor constantly putting the needs of the narcissist above their own, often to their own detriment.

Empathy, on the other hand, is a positive trait that involves the ability to deeply understand and share the feelings of others. Empaths are naturally compassionate individuals who want to help and nurture those they love. However, when they fail to establish proper boundaries, their empathy can be exploited. Narcissists, drawn to empathetic individuals because of their desire for control, will often use the victim's kindness, empathy, and compassion as tools for manipulation. They will guilt the empath into sacrificing their own needs, leading them to lose sight of their personal boundaries and sense of self.

Many narcissistic abuse survivors grapple with feelings of guilt when they assert themselves or try to create distance. They may feel selfish or unloving for setting boundaries, believing that to love someone means to put their needs first, even when it's detrimental to their own mental health. This false sense of responsibility to the narcissist's well-being only deepens the survivor's sense of emotional instability and confusion. It's important to recognize that having empathy does not mean being obligated to sacrifice your well-being for the sake of someone else. Setting boundaries and protecting your emotional space is a key part of healing.

The Psychological Toll: Self-Doubt and Gaslighting

One of the most insidious aspects of narcissistic abuse is gaslighting, where the abuser manipulates the victim into doubting their own perceptions, memories, and judgments. This creates an environment where the survivor constantly questions themselves and their reality. Narcissists often use this tactic to avoid accountability, making it harder for the victim to see the abuse for what it is.

Survivors may begin to ask themselves questions like, "Am I overreacting?" "Did I really say that?" "Was I too sensitive?" Narcissists will often deny events, manipulate conversations, or make you feel like you're crazy for pointing out their behavior. The result is a slow erosion of confidence and trust in one's own judgment, which can manifest as self-doubt. This self-doubt affects not only the survivor's relationship with the narcissist but can extend to their relationships with others as well. They may begin to second-guess everything—from their personal decisions to their friendships, careers, and beyond.

As this cycle of doubt continues, the survivor can feel as though they are losing touch with who they once were. They may withdraw from friends, family, or work, as they become too emotionally exhausted to maintain any semblance of normalcy. The narcissist's consistent denial and minimization of their actions further exacerbate the survivor's confusion, leading them to question their own worth and integrity.

The Emotional Fallout: Anger, Isolation, and Behavioral Changes

The emotional fallout of narcissistic abuse doesn't just manifest as confusion or self-doubt; it also triggers a range of negative emotions. Survivors may begin to experience anger, frustration, or resentment—feelings that may have previously been foreign to them. These emotions are often a result of the survivor realizing, often too late, that their once-loving partner is emotionally unavailable or even cruel.

This anger is not just directed toward the narcissist but also toward themselves for not recognizing the signs sooner or for feeling trapped in a relationship that drains them emotionally. The survivor may also feel guilt for having allowed themselves to be manipulated for so long, and for not standing up for themselves earlier in the relationship.

As these emotions fester, survivors may begin to act out of character, which further contributes to their self-alienation. They might begin using tactics they previously abhorred—like silent treatment, passive aggression, or even manipulation—to communicate their pain or frustration. This is a defense mechanism, a learned behavior that survivors adopt as a way to protect themselves. However, this shift in behavior doesn't change the narcissist; it reflects the emotional and psychological toll the abuse has had on the survivor.

The behavioral changes that come with narcissistic abuse are often misinterpreted by others, leading to further isolation and misunderstanding. Friends and family might think the survivor is becoming difficult or emotionally volatile, not understanding that these behaviors are a response to years of emotional trauma.

Regaining Self-Worth: The Path to Healing

The process of healing from narcissistic abuse involves rediscovering who you are and reclaiming the parts of yourself that the abuse has tried to take away. A crucial part of this healing is recognizing the damage the abuse has caused. It's vital to validate your own feelings and experiences rather than minimizing the harm that's been done to you.

Survivors often minimize the severity of the abuse, dismissing it as "not that bad" or "I should have been stronger." This self-doubt is a natural outcome of gaslighting and narcissistic manipulation. It's important to acknowledge the emotional abuse and give yourself the compassion you deserve. Recovery starts when you allow yourself to feel the full range of emotions—anger, sadness, grief—without shame or guilt.

Part of healing involves regaining trust in your own judgment and learning to set healthy boundaries. This means reestablishing a sense of self by saying no when needed, rejecting manipulative behavior, and learning to care for yourself as you would a loved one. Healing is a gradual process, but it begins with taking small steps toward reclaiming your identity and sense of worth.

Survivors of narcissistic abuse deserve to feel whole again, to rediscover the strength and resilience that were there all along. It's a journey that takes time, but it is one that's absolutely worth undertaking. Embrace your healing, knowing that the road ahead is full of potential and that you are worthy of love, respect, and happiness.

CHAPTER FOUR

EMOTIONAL DISTRESS

"Through emotional distress, each step forward is a courageous act of reclaiming your strength and finding your way back to hope."

The emotional turmoil that comes from experiencing narcissistic abuse can be overwhelming and often hard to pinpoint. Many individuals who seek therapy after enduring psychological abuse don't immediately recognize it as abuse; they just know that something in their lives feels deeply wrong. The feelings are often too complex and overwhelming to describe—like a persistent ache that refuses to go away. If you've been through this type of trauma, you might find yourself wondering, "Why do I feel so anxious, depressed, or confused?" The truth is, narcissistic abuse leaves an emotional imprint that can drastically alter how you see yourself and the world. This chapter explores the emotional distress caused by narcissistic abuse and how therapy can help survivors navigate the painful journey to healing.

Stepping Into Therapy: A Cloud of Confusion

Imagine walking into a therapy room, unsure of where to begin or how to explain the turmoil that has become your life. Survivors of narcissistic abuse often arrive at therapy feeling lost. They may have spent months or years in a relationship where their sense of self was chipped away, and they're now struggling to understand why they feel emotionally exhausted, anxious, or overwhelmed. Many might feel like they're losing touch with who they once were—becoming strangers to themselves. In the beginning, it can be difficult to even articulate the cause of this distress.

For the therapist, the first priority is to create a safe and nonjudgmental space where the survivor can express their feelings freely. This initial phase of therapy can be difficult. Opening up about the pain, confusion, and despair caused by narcissistic abuse can trigger painful memories and emotions. But as therapy progresses, there's often a flicker of hope, like the first rays of sunlight piercing through a stormy sky. Survivors slowly start to connect the dots between their emotional distress and the abusive patterns they've endured.

Safety First: Assessing Risks

One of the first things a therapist will do when working with a survivor of narcissistic abuse is to assess their emotional and psychological safety. Abuse, whether physical, emotional, or psychological, can sometimes create such severe feelings of despair that the survivor contemplates self-harm or even suicide. The overwhelming feeling of worthlessness that comes from constant emotional manipulation and criticism can be devastating. Survivors may internalize the abuse to the point where they believe they are unworthy of love, happiness, or even life itself.

If you are reading this and struggling with feelings of hopelessness or thoughts of self-harm, please understand that reaching out for help is crucial. Contact a therapist, call a crisis hotline, or speak to a trusted friend or family member. Asking for help is not a sign of weakness; it's a testament to your strength and courage to reclaim your life.

Once the therapist ensures there is no immediate risk to the survivor's safety, the deeper work begins. The therapist will help the individual explore the layers of despair they are feeling and begin unpacking the abusive experiences that led them to this point. These sessions often reveal the profound impact of emotional and psychological abuse, where the victim's feelings of self-worth have been eroded to the point of near collapse.

Unpacking Experiences and Patterns

As therapy unfolds, the therapist will help the survivor connect the dots between their emotional distress and the patterns of abuse they've endured. Narcissistic abuse often begins subtly—small moments of manipulation or criticism that may seem like ordinary relationship problems. At first, the victim may not recognize these behaviors as abuse. They might even blame themselves, thinking that "everyone has arguments" or that their partner's actions are just part of a "rough patch." This initial confusion can be exacerbated by the narcissist's love-bombing—showing affection and kindness after a particularly cruel episode, which creates a confusing emotional cycle.

In therapy, survivors are guided to identify the patterns of manipulation and control that often go unnoticed in the moment. For example, the narcissist might use affection or kindness as a tool for manipulation. They may shower the victim with compliments or affection after a period of cruelty, creating a sense of hope that things will get better. This "hope and despair" cycle can keep the survivor trapped in the relationship, desperately clinging to the good moments while denying the toxic ones.

As therapy helps uncover these patterns, survivors begin to understand that the emotional distress they've been feeling is not their fault. They're not "too sensitive" or "too dramatic." Instead, they've been subjected to consistent emotional manipulation by someone skilled at exploiting their vulnerabilities. The therapist's role is to help the survivor break free from this confusion and validate their experiences, helping them see the abuse for what it is.

The Despair Stage: Self-Doubt and Emotional Exhaustion

When survivors of narcissistic abuse first come to therapy, they often find themselves in what is called the Despair Stage. This stage is characterized by emotional exhaustion, sadness, and an overwhelming sense of hopelessness. Survivors may feel that no matter what they do, they can never please their abuser or make the relationship work. The constant criticism, gaslighting, and emotional manipulation leave them questioning their own worth, making them believe they are inherently flawed or unlovable.

It's common for survivors to replay past events in their minds, wondering where they went wrong. They may think, "If only I had been better," or "If I had tried harder, maybe things wouldn't have turned out this way." This self-blame is one of the most damaging consequences of narcissistic abuse. It clouds their perception of the situation and distracts them from recognizing the true source of their pain: the abuser's harmful behavior.

In therapy, survivors are encouraged to challenge these false beliefs and start seeing the manipulation for what it is. The narcissist's behavior is not a reflection of the survivor's worth, but a direct consequence of the narcissist's desire to control and devalue others. Survivors often need to be reminded repeatedly that they are not to blame for the abuse they've suffered.

Challenging False Beliefs: Reclaiming Reality

One of the most important steps in the therapeutic process is challenging the false beliefs that the narcissist has instilled in the survivor. Narcissists often use psychological tactics like gaslighting, projection, and devaluation to distort the victim's perception of reality. They may tell the survivor they're "too sensitive," "overreacting," or "imagining things," which leads the victim to question their own emotions and experiences.

Therapists work with survivors to identify these false beliefs and dismantle them, helping the individual reclaim their sense of reality. It's like peeling away layers of deceit to reveal the truth: the survivor's feelings are valid, and their experiences are real. Overcoming this gaslighting is a critical part of the healing process. It allows survivors to regain trust in their own perceptions and start believing in their inherent worth again.

As survivors challenge these false beliefs, they also begin to see that the love and affection shown by the narcissist after moments of cruelty were not genuine but part of a manipulation tactic. The narcissist's kindness was often a tool used to maintain control and keep the survivor emotionally dependent. Recognizing this is empowering, as it helps survivors break free from the emotional cycle of abuse.

Taking It One Step at a Time: Patience and Progress

Healing from narcissistic abuse is not an overnight process. It is a journey that requires patience, self-compassion, and a willingness to take small steps forward. Survivors may find themselves asking questions like, "Why does this still hurt so much?" or "Am I ever going to feel like myself again?" These are normal questions, but they don't have easy answers. Recovery takes time.

The therapist will help the survivor set realistic goals for healing, focusing on gradual progress rather than expecting immediate results. The emotional distress that comes from narcissistic abuse can be overwhelming, but with each small step—whether it's setting a boundary, speaking up for oneself, or simply acknowledging the pain—the survivor moves closer to reclaiming their life.

It's important to recognize that healing is not linear. Some days will feel better than others, and there may be setbacks. But each step forward, no matter how small, is an important part of the process. Survivors are encouraged to celebrate their progress, even the smallest victories. For example, setting a boundary with an abusive friend or partner can be a huge accomplishment, signaling a shift toward reclaiming control over their own life.

Harnessing Anger for Change

One emotion that often surfaces during the healing process is anger. Anger can be a powerful force for change when channeled appropriately. It's a natural response to being mistreated and manipulated for so long. However, survivors often feel guilty for their anger, thinking that they should be forgiving or that it's wrong to feel upset after what they've been through.

Therapists help survivors understand that anger, when processed healthily, can be a motivating force for change. Instead of suppressing anger, survivors can channel it into productive actions, such as writing about their experiences, journaling, or creating a vision board for their future. Physical activities like exercise or yoga can also help release built-up tension and provide emotional relief.

Embracing the Healing Journey

Healing from narcissistic abuse is a deeply personal journey, one that unfolds over time. It's about reclaiming your voice, rediscovering your worth, and building a future that is free from manipulation and control. Throughout this journey, survivors should surround themselves with supportive people—friends, family, or online communities who truly understand their pain.

The path to recovery may seem daunting at times, but with the right support, tools, and mindset, it is absolutely possible to heal. Every step taken is a victory, and each small change moves the survivor closer to a future filled with hope, joy, and empowerment. Remember: you are not alone, and healing is within reach.

LEARNING

"Awareness is the first step toward freedom; understanding the unseen tactics of emotional manipulation lights the path to healing."

Psychological abuse, especially in relationships with narcissists, can feel like an invisible force, quietly and powerfully controlling your life. Often, those who experience this type of abuse find it hard to express or even recognize what's happening. They might feel confused, disoriented, and unsure of what is real and what isn't. In many ways, the emotional chaos and psychological manipulation that comes with narcissistic abuse leave survivors struggling to make sense of their experiences.

The good news is that understanding the tactics used by narcissistic abusers can provide much-needed clarity. Recognizing the psychological manipulation that has been at play is the first step toward healing. This chapter explores the tactics of narcissistic abuse and how learning about them can empower survivors to regain control, rebuild their sense of self, and avoid falling into similar patterns in the future.

The Cycle of Narcissistic Abuse: A Trap of Emotional Turmoil

The relationship with a narcissist typically follows a recognizable pattern that traps individuals in a cycle of emotional turmoil. This cycle is not always immediately apparent, and many survivors describe feeling like they were in an emotional whirlwind—one moment being treated as a special and cherished partner, and the next being devalued or discarded. This emotional rollercoaster is known as the cycle of narcissistic abuse, and it often consists of four main stages: Love Bombing, Devaluation, Discard, and Hoovering.

By understanding this cycle, survivors can start to untangle the confusion and chaos that defines their relationships with narcissists. This newfound awareness can be both validating and empowering, allowing survivors to break free from the patterns of abuse and regain control of their emotional lives.

Love Bombing: The Illusion of Perfection

In the beginning, narcissists often seem like the perfect partner. This phase is called love bombing, where the narcissist showers the victim with an overwhelming amount of affection, praise, and attention. They may appear almost too good to be true, mirroring the victim's interests and values, making them feel understood and cherished.

Imagine meeting someone who seems to know you inside and out, someone who instantly connects with everything you care about. If you love hiking, for example, they might suddenly become an avid hiker too, showing up with new gear and an infectious excitement about your shared hobby. This kind of attention feels exhilarating, creating an intoxicating emotional bond.

At first, it can feel like you've found your soulmate—someone who makes you feel seen, valued, and even adored. However, this intense affection is usually a carefully constructed act. The narcissist is not genuinely interested in you as a person; they are interested in the version of you that feeds their own ego and fulfills their emotional needs. In many ways, love bombing is a form of manipulation, designed to hook you in and create a sense of emotional dependency.

For the survivor, this initial phase can be disorienting because they may feel swept up in the whirlwind of affection and validation. The problem is that this love is often conditional, based not on mutual respect, but on the narcissist's desire to maintain control. The affection may disappear as quickly as it came, leaving you feeling confused and abandoned.

Devaluation: The Shift That Shatters Your Self-Worth

Once the narcissist has fully hooked you with their charm, the dynamics of the relationship begin to change. The devaluation phase sets in when the narcissist starts to withdraw affection and replace it with criticism, neglect, and emotional manipulation.

This stage is deeply painful because it involves a stark shift from the intense adoration of the initial phase. The narcissist may suddenly become distant or even openly critical. They might belittle your achievements, mock your vulnerabilities, or undermine your confidence in subtle ways. If you share a personal insecurity—say, you feel self-conscious about your career or your appearance—they may exploit that vulnerability to further tear you down, making you feel inadequate or unworthy.

The emotional withdrawal can also manifest in dismissive behaviors like ignoring your texts or avoiding spending time with you. When you do manage to get their attention, it may feel cold or distant. The narcissist may give you the silent treatment or belittle you for needing their validation. You might start questioning what you've done wrong, constantly seeking to earn their approval again. This cycle of emotional up and down is exhausting and disorienting, leading you to feel lost, anxious, and unsure of who you are.

In this stage, the narcissist may also attempt to isolate you from friends and family, making you feel as though you're the problem or that no one else understands you. The gaslighting can be intense, with the narcissist twisting your words or making you feel like you're overreacting. You might find yourself thinking, "If I just show them I care more, if I just do more, maybe they will love me again."

The devaluation stage is where you may start to feel deeply confused and self-doubting. It's important to remember that this shift is a manipulation tactic, designed to make you feel powerless and dependent. The narcissist thrives on your emotional insecurity, as it makes it easier for them to maintain control.

Discard: The Abrupt Ending

When the narcissist decides that you're no longer serving their needs, the discard phase can occur. This is the moment when the narcissist abruptly ends the relationship, often without any explanation. The victim is left in a state of emotional shock, bewildered by the sudden turn of events.

The discard can be as harsh as it is sudden. In some cases, the narcissist may even push the victim to end things in a way that preserves their own image, leaving the victim questioning what they did wrong. It's common to feel abandoned, betrayed, and emotionally devastated during this phase. The narcissist may have already lined up a new partner, grooming them while still involved with you, making the break-up feel even more jarring.

At this stage, many victims are left wondering, "What happened? Where did the love go?" These feelings of abandonment can be exacerbated by the realization that the narcissist has already moved on, leaving the victim alone and emotionally shattered. This abruptness can leave the survivor feeling empty, confused, and desperate for closure.

Hoovering: The Return of the Narcissist

Just when the victim believes they have escaped the narcissist's grip, they may experience a phenomenon known as hoovering. This term, named after the vacuum cleaner, refers to the narcissist's attempt to "suck" the victim back into the relationship after the discard. Hoovering can take many forms, but it often involves the narcissist suddenly resurfacing, offering apologies, promising to change, or trying to rekindle the intense affection of the early days.

For example, they might text you with a message that says, "I've been thinking about you a lot. I miss our late-night talks," or "I know I messed up, but I've changed." These grand gestures or heartfelt promises can feel incredibly tempting, making you question whether they've truly changed. The narcissist may also try to appeal to your emotions, reminding you of the good times and manipulating your sense of nostalgia.

However, this attempt to reel you back in is nothing more than a manipulation tactic. The narcissist is not genuinely sorry or committed to change; they simply want to regain control and continue feeding their ego at your expense. If you resist their advances, the narcissist may react with anger or frustration, resorting to tactics like smear campaigns (trying to damage your reputation) or gaslighting (making you question your own perception of reality).

At this point, survivors may feel caught between wanting to believe the narcissist's promises and recognizing the toxic cycle they're stuck in. This internal battle is exhausting, and often the only way to break free is by firmly setting boundaries and refusing to engage with the narcissist's manipulative behaviors.

Gaining Clarity: Understanding the Cycle of Narcissistic Abuse

Recognizing the cycle of narcissistic abuse is crucial for survivors. It helps explain the confusion, self-doubt, and emotional pain that often accompany abusive relationships. By understanding that love bombing, devaluation, discard, and hoovering are all part of the narcissist's manipulation tactics, survivors can start to regain a sense of clarity. This knowledge validates the feelings that may have once seemed irrational or hard to explain.

It's empowering to realize that you were not the cause of the chaos and that the cycle of abuse is a deliberate strategy designed to control and manipulate you. With this understanding, survivors can begin to take steps toward healing.

Moving Forward: Building Healthier Relationships

The lessons learned from narcissistic abuse, though painful, can ultimately help survivors build healthier relationships in the future. By identifying the red flags—such as someone who is too eager to impress or who dismisses your feelings—you can better protect yourself from falling into toxic dynamics again.

Healing from narcissistic abuse also involves rebuilding self-worth. It's essential to surround yourself with people who respect, value, and support you. Focus on rediscovering your passions, engaging in activities that bring you joy, and learning to trust yourself again. Each step toward self-love is a step toward healing.

Narcissistic abuse leaves deep emotional scars, but understanding the tactics involved and how they were used to control you is the first step toward regaining your life and rebuilding your sense of self. With time, patience, and the right support, you can move beyond the shadows of the narcissistic cycle and embrace a future filled with healthier, more fulfilling relationships.

In the end, healing from narcissistic abuse is not just about recognizing what went wrong; it's about reclaiming your power, learning from your experiences, and moving forward with strength and resilience. You are not defined by your past, but by your ability to grow, heal, and rebuild your life.

CHAPTER SIX

COMMON EXPERIENCES

"Your story may feel unique, but many share the same
threads of confusion and pain; recognizing this connection
is the first step toward healing."

Narcissistic abuse is a silent, insidious form of emotional manipulation that can infiltrate every corner of life—whether in a personal relationship or at work. The manipulation techniques narcissists use are designed to control, devalue, and dominate their victims. The emotional toll they take can be devastating, leaving the victim feeling powerless, confused, and emotionally drained. Understanding the common tactics used by narcissists is vital to recognizing these behaviors and breaking free from their grasp.

One of the most common tactics narcissists use to manipulate their victims is gaslighting—a psychological tool that makes you question your own reality. Imagine having a conversation about attending an event with a partner. When the day arrives, they insist they never agreed to it, claiming that you must be misremembering the details. This subtle distortion of reality makes you start doubting yourself, leading to confusion and self-doubt. Over time, gaslighting erodes your sense of certainty, causing you to second-guess your own memories and perceptions. The narcissist succeeds in making you question whether you're the one who is wrong, even when you know deep down that you're not.

Narcissists are also notorious for lying, and they do it with ease. These lies are often not just for convenience but to manipulate situations to their advantage. A partner might promise to handle something important, like taking care of a chore or making a decision together, only to later deny ever making the promise. Instead of owning up to it, they'll insist that you're mistaken, shifting the blame onto you for misunderstanding. These lies are often so convincing that you might start doubting your own memory or judgment. In a work environment, a colleague or boss might deny having asked you to take on a particular task, despite having had clear discussions about it. The lies they tell can leave you feeling trapped in a constant cycle of trying to determine what is real and what is fabricated.

Another classic narcissistic tactic is withholding—withholding affection, communication, or even basic information to punish and control. In personal relationships, this can manifest as emotional withdrawal. For instance, after a disagreement, your partner might suddenly stop being affectionate, or they might ignore you entirely, refusing to engage in conversation. You haven't done anything wrong, but they choose to pull away emotionally as a way to manipulate you into feeling isolated or rejected. At work, withholding information is a tactic used by narcissistic bosses or coworkers who don't want to share critical details that would make your job easier. They might refuse to give you clear instructions or delay offering feedback, leaving you floundering in uncertainty. This lack of communication forces you to depend on them, creating an emotional power imbalance.

Perhaps one of the most invasive forms of manipulation is stalking. After a relationship ends or when a narcissist feels that they are losing control, they may resort to following you around, checking your social media accounts, or even showing up uninvited at places they know you frequent. Their sense of entitlement and obsession with knowing everything about you keeps them in your life, even when you've tried to distance yourself. This kind of behavior is invasive and can be terrifying, especially if they try to justify it by claiming that they "just wanted to make sure you're okay." In the workplace, stalking can take the form of surveillance, where a narcissistic boss or coworker might keep a close eye on your every move—observing how you interact with others, tracking your work hours, or constantly checking on your progress in an attempt to maintain control.

A particularly dangerous tactic is future faking, where the narcissist makes grand promises about an idealized future—promises of vacations, future plans, or commitments to better behavior that never come to fruition. For example, a narcissistic partner might talk excitedly about plans for a future vacation, buying a house together, or even starting a family, making you feel as though you're working toward something amazing. However, when the time arrives, those promises are always delayed or forgotten, leaving you constantly hoping for something that may never materialize. At work, narcissistic bosses often use future faking to keep their employees motivated. They might dangle promises of a raise, promotion, or new responsibilities to keep you working hard, only to fail to deliver when the time comes. These false promises leave you emotionally attached to a future that will never come.

Triangulation is another manipulation strategy that involves introducing a third party to stir up jealousy, insecurity, and confusion. In relationships, a narcissistic partner might frequently bring up an ex in conversation, comparing you to them or even flirting with someone else in front of you. They might say things like, "My ex was always so good at doing this for me," or "I wish you were more like them." These remarks are meant to create doubt in your mind and make you feel inadequate. At work, triangulation can happen when a narcissistic colleague constantly praises another coworker's work in front of you or pits you against someone else by drawing comparisons. The goal is to make you feel like you're in competition for their attention or approval, keeping you emotionally destabilized and constantly trying to prove your worth.

If a narcissist senses that you're beginning to pull away or are losing interest, they might engage in breadcrumbing—giving you just enough attention to keep you invested in the relationship or situation. This could mean a few affectionate gestures or promises to change, but the efforts are always half-hearted. In a personal relationship, breadcrumbing might look like a partner sending a few sweet messages after weeks of neglect or making grandiose promises that never materialize. At work, breadcrumbing can happen when a boss or manager gives you occasional praise but never follows through with any concrete rewards or recognition. They may offer just enough praise to keep you hooked but fail to offer any real support or advancement.

Cheating is another tactic narcissists often use as a way of seeking validation and attention from multiple sources. In a relationship, a narcissistic partner may cheat without remorse, using their need for external validation as a way to fuel their ego. When confronted, they might deny the cheating or turn the blame on you for being too controlling or insecure. At work, a narcissist might cheat by taking credit for others' ideas or projects. They might present your work as their own during a meeting, leaving you to watch as they bask in the glory of your efforts. If confronted, they will likely deny their actions, twisting the narrative and shifting blame onto you. In both cases, their need for validation outweighs any sense of loyalty or ethical behavior.

The constant need for control is a hallmark of narcissistic behavior. Whether in marriage or at work, narcissists crave dominance over every aspect of their victim's life. In a marriage, they might try to control how you spend your time, what you wear, who you associate with, or even what you eat. Their criticism of your choices, whether subtle or overt, is meant to reinforce their authority and make you feel that your decisions are never good enough. At work, narcissistic bosses may micromanage every aspect of your work, from how you communicate with coworkers to how you handle tasks. They may dictate when you take breaks or criticize your performance over the smallest details, even if the larger goals are being met.

Stonewalling is another tactic that narcissists use to avoid taking responsibility. When you try to discuss a problem, express your feelings, or address a boundary that's been crossed, they simply shut down and refuse to engage. This could involve ignoring you completely, giving you a blank stare, or walking away in the middle of a conversation. At work, a narcissistic boss might stonewall you when you ask for help or clarification on a project, leaving you feeling unsupported and frustrated. By refusing to communicate, they maintain control of the situation and avoid any accountability for their actions or words.

Finally, the silent treatment is another form of punishment used by narcissists to make you feel rejected and powerless. When they are angry or upset with you, they may refuse to speak to you for days on end, leaving you scrambling to figure out what you did wrong. This form of emotional abuse creates feelings of isolation and despair, making you desperate for their attention and approval. At work, a narcissistic colleague or boss might ignore your contributions or deliberately exclude you from important meetings, leaving you feeling invisible and unappreciated.

CHAPTER SEVEN

REALIZATION

"Awakening to the truth is both a painful and powerful journey; it is the moment you reclaim your voice and begin to heal."

When survivors of psychological abuse begin to recognize their suffering and learn about the ways abusers manipulate and harm others, they often experience what is known as an awakening. This moment marks a pivotal shift in their understanding of their experiences, leading to breakthrough realizations. It's during this time that many survivors start to articulate their pain, learn new terminology, and feel a sense of connection with others who have shared similar journeys.

The Rollercoaster of Emotions

As survivors navigate this awakening, it's not uncommon for them to cycle between feelings of empowerment and despair. This emotional ebb and flow is a normal part of recovery. Anger, in particular, often emerges during this stage, as survivors confront the reality of what they've endured. They may find themselves expressing powerful sentiments such as:

- "I'm not crazy."
- "What happened to me has a name, and others understand it too."
- "I know now that evil exists."
- "I was made to think it was my fault."
- "I can't believe they did this to me."

This phase is fundamentally about finding your voice and grappling with the reality of the abuse. It can be intense and emotional, pushing survivors to ask hard questions: "How could they treat me like this?"

The Complexity of Clarity

Recognizing the dynamics of psychological abuse can be challenging but is essential for healing. Survivors often experience moments of clarity, followed by confusion as they confront the truth of their past. It's common to feel empowered one moment and then miss the abuser the next. Many survivors struggle with the urge to make excuses for their abuser's behavior, often attributing it to past trauma or mental illness. However, grasping the reality that toxic individuals lack empathy is crucial for letting go of these justifications and moving forward.

The Importance of Describing the Abuse

During this awakening, describing the abuse becomes a vital part of the healing process. It allows survivors to communicate their pain more effectively and begin to make sense of their experiences. As they articulate their feelings, many find themselves becoming more settled and regaining a sense of strength. They may have moments of clarity in everyday decisions, realizing just how controlled they once were.

Connecting with Community

Connecting with other survivors can provide invaluable support during this time. Online communities and resources offer spaces where individuals can share their experiences and find solace among peers who understand their journey. If you haven't explored these options, it could be beneficial to do so. Just be mindful of trolls and prioritize groups that foster a supportive environment for recovery.

In-person support groups can also be incredibly valuable. They create safe spaces for survivors to share their stories and connect with others who have walked similar paths. The camaraderie found in these groups can remind survivors that they are not alone in their struggle, helping to reinforce their healing journey.

The awakening is a powerful and transformative stage in the recovery process. While it can be marked by intense emotions and confusion, it ultimately leads to greater self-awareness and empowerment. By acknowledging the truth of their experiences, finding their voice, and connecting with supportive communities, survivors take vital steps toward reclaiming their lives. Remember, the journey is not linear, and it's perfectly normal to oscillate between clarity and doubt. Embrace the process, and know that healing is within reach

BOUNDARIES

"Boundaries are the bridge to reclaiming your life; they honor your needs while defining what you will no longer accept."

After a survivor has identified their despair, learned about psychological abuse, realized recovery is possible, and set boundaries, the next step is Recovery. This means working to regain what was lost during the abuse, such as material possessions, financial stability, physical health, or mental well-being.

Recovery can take time, so it's important to be patient. This stage is marked by survivors starting to focus on activities outside of recovery work, like exploring new hobbies and enjoying life. This shift indicates they're ready to move forward.

A common obstacle is the fear that moving on means letting the abuser off the hook. However, moving forward doesn't erase the abuse—it simply means the survivor is reclaiming their life. It's about showing that the abuse didn't destroy them beyond repair.

Recovery might involve:

- Enjoying holidays and celebrations again.
- Regaining financial stability by paying off debts and saving.
- Improving physical health, like reducing pain and increasing energy.
- Enhancing emotional well-being by reducing anxiety and depression.
- Replacing material items lost or damaged during the abuse.

Survivors can't get back lost time, but they can work on improving their lives. This stage is about turning what was lost into new opportunities for joy and growth. It's not about perfection but about finding ways to make life better and more fulfilling. If you feel overwhelmed, take breaks and return to your recovery efforts with hope and patience.

Enjoying Special Moments

When recovering from psychological abuse, survivors often find that holidays, vacations, and other special events were ruined by toxic people. This happens because these individuals are uncomfortable with closeness and teamwork, leading them to create chaos to push others away. They often ruin special days like birthdays or holidays because they can't stand attention being away from them.

Recovery means reclaiming these special moments. If you've cut contact with the abuser, try celebrating in a new way, even if it's just treating yourself to something small like a meal out or a bouquet of flowers. This shows that you value special occasions, despite the abuser's past impact.

When planning future trips, keep your expectations realistic and focus on what you can control, like enjoying moments of solitude and the joy of getting away from routine. Shorter trips may be easier than longer ones, helping you avoid potential conflict with the abuser.

Financial Stability

Financial abuse is common and comes in two forms:

1. Creating Dependency: The abuser makes the survivor financially dependent to control them. This can involve sabotaging their financial independence or creating a reliance under the guise of care.

2. Entitlement: The abuser uses the survivor's financial resources for their own needs, often refusing to contribute fairly to the household.

Recovery in finances means taking small steps to regain control. Start by listing your financial issues and taking tiny steps toward improvement. For example, open a savings account and set up a small automatic transfer. Even a small amount can build momentum and lead to bigger changes over time.

Physical Health and Emotional Well-being Recovery

Physical Health:

Psychological abuse often causes physical health issues. Stress from such abuse can lead to conditions like autoimmune disorders, chronic inflammation, and body pain. Recovery involves acknowledging and addressing these health impacts. Start by getting a full physical check-up and discussing any symptoms with your doctor. If you're not a fan of conventional medicine, consider alternative treatments like Ayurveda or massage therapy.

Exercise is also important but should be gentle at first. Instead of intense workouts, try short, manageable sessions like 20-minute walks or moderate yoga. As you rebuild your energy, gradually increase your activity level. Consistency, not intensity, is key at this stage. Exercise can improve both your physical and mental health, so aim for regular, light activities to boost your mood and overall well-being.

Emotional Well-being:

Psychological abuse can mask or worsen depression and anxiety. The adrenaline from toxic relationships might temporarily lift your mood, but recovery requires addressing the underlying issues. During the Restoration stage, focus on recalibrating your emotions. This process takes time and involves finding what genuinely helps you feel better.

Identify activities and habits that improve your emotional health and avoid those that don't. Your goal is to replace old, harmful patterns with new, positive ones. Embrace moments of joy and laughter, and allow yourself to experience authentic happiness. Recovery from emotional distress will come in waves, but gradually, the good days will outweigh the bad ones.

In summary, focus on gentle physical activities and discover what enriches your emotional health. This stage of recovery is about finding balance and allowing yourself to heal in a way that suits your needs.

Replacing Items Lost During Abuse

Restoring material items lost or destroyed during abuse is a crucial part of healing. For example, someone might have had a treasured medal or personal item destroyed by an abuser. This item might have held significant sentimental value, symbolizing past achievements or cherished memories.

When faced with such losses, it's important to think about what items were meaningful to you but were lost or damaged during the abuse. Did your abuser force you to give up a beloved pet or alter your personal style? Maybe you lost a piece of artwork that was special to you. Identifying these losses is the first step in finding ways to replace or create new items and memories that bring you joy.

Restoring material items can involve finding new ways to commemorate past achievements or replacing items that had emotional significance. For instance, if you had a cherished award or piece of art that was lost, you might seek out a new award or create a new piece of art that reflects your current life and recovery.

However, it's important to recognize that not everything can be fully restored. Some losses, such as irreplaceable items or past relationships, might remain as they are. Accepting these realities is a part of the healing process.

The key is to focus on reclaiming what you can and creating new, meaningful experiences. While you may not be able to restore everything, taking steps to replace or recreate important items can support your recovery and help you move forward.

CHAPTER NINE

DIFFICULT THINGS TO BELIEVE

"Sometimes the hardest truths to accept are the very ones that set us free."

Even after being educated about the behavior of narcissistic abusers, it's common to struggle with fully accepting that such people truly exist in the world. You might think of a friend's ex as just a little cocky, maybe a bit annoying at times—but overall, they might seem friendly or even kind on occasion. However, when you step back and truly consider the pattern of behavior described, it becomes clear that narcissistic abuse is not only real, but the damage it causes can be deep and long-lasting. If a loved one shares stories of suffering at the hands of an abuser, it's important to take those experiences seriously—even if the narcissist in question sometimes appears charming, likable, or even harmless on the surface.

Understanding narcissistic behavior can be a challenge, and for someone on the outside looking in, it may seem nearly impossible to believe that someone could behave in such hurtful, manipulative ways. This chapter explores the hard-to-believe aspects of narcissistic abuse, helping you gain a deeper understanding of why these relationships are so damaging. When you start to truly grasp these realities, you can better support loved ones who have been through this kind of trauma and begin to understand how difficult it can be for survivors to break free.

The Self-Centered Nature of Narcissists

One of the most difficult things to come to terms with is the narcissist's lack of genuine care for others. Narcissists are primarily concerned with their own needs, desires, and egos. They may appear friendly or engaging, but their interest in others is never truly selfless. If they are showing interest or affection, it is likely because your presence serves a purpose for them—whether it boosts their ego, provides them with validation, or fulfills some other selfish need. In their eyes, relationships are transactional. The "narcissistic supply"—a term used to describe the emotional or psychological fuel narcissists get from others—is the only thing that sustains them. They need constant praise and attention to maintain their inflated self-image, and this makes them often cruelly indifferent to the feelings or well-being of others.

For someone who has never experienced a narcissistic relationship, it can be difficult to accept just how surface-level their connections are. Narcissists often struggle to form deep, mutual relationships. They may seem charming at first, but as time goes on, their lack of emotional reciprocity becomes apparent. When their partners or friends try to express their needs, the narcissist either disregards them or twists them to suit their own interests. The shallow connections they form leave those around them feeling unfulfilled, used, and emotionally drained.

The most painful truth for survivors to accept is the fact that narcissists cannot truly love anyone. This is a difficult concept because it goes against everything we expect in relationships. Love, compassion, empathy—these qualities are supposed to be the bedrock of healthy human connections. But for narcissists, those emotions are often missing. Their emotional framework revolves entirely around themselves. They view others through a lens of what they can provide or how they make the narcissist feel about themselves. The idea of loving someone unconditionally is foreign to them. As such, they can never offer the depth of connection or mutual care that a healthy relationship provides.

The Facade of Narcissists

Another challenging aspect of narcissistic abuse is the illusion of the person you think you know. Many narcissists are incredibly adept at creating different personas that allow them to gain the attention and admiration they crave. This is especially true in the early stages of a relationship, when they will present an idealized version of themselves to win you over. They are like actors, playing the role that they believe will best serve their interests, often molding their personality to match your desires, values, and interests.

For instance, a narcissistic partner may present themselves as the perfect, thoughtful, kind individual who always seems to know exactly what to say. They may shower you with affection, compliments, and promises of a beautiful future together. In these early days, it can feel like you've met your soulmate. However, as the relationship progresses, the cracks in their persona begin to show. The perfect partner turns out to be a facade, a carefully constructed image meant to manipulate you into providing them with attention, admiration, or other forms of narcissistic supply.

This creates a cycle of emotional confusion, because the person you fell in love with—or the friend you thought you could trust—may not even exist. This is one of the most painful aspects of narcissistic abuse: the realization that the connection you had with the narcissist was based on a lie. Their attention-seeking behavior is a calculated move, always designed to enhance their image, not reflect any real, selfless concern for you or your well-being. Everything they do, whether it's being kind or helpful, is a tactic to maintain control and admiration. Their actions may seem selfless, but they are driven by the need for validation, rather than love or care.

The Dynamics of Narcissistic Relationships

The relationship dynamics that narcissists create are complex, and they often leave their partners feeling emotionally drained and confused. Narcissists are drawn to people who possess qualities they feel they lack—such as success, kindness, or positivity—and will often use these partners to boost their own self-esteem. The attraction isn't about love or mutual respect; it's about using the other person as a tool for emotional self-aggrandizement. Your friend's ex may have been drawn to their qualities, and once they were in the relationship, they used their partner's strengths to prop themselves up, all while leaving their partner emotionally exhausted.

A common behavior in narcissistic relationships is possessiveness. Narcissists often treat their partners like property—something to own and control. After an intense period of love bombing and emotional manipulation, the narcissist may feel a deep sense of entitlement to their partner. They might use possessive behaviors, such as tracking their partner's movements, limiting their access to friends, or making decisions for them. These controlling actions are designed to keep the partner emotionally dependent on the narcissist, while the narcissist secures a source of emotional supply.

If the partner tries to set boundaries or leave the relationship, the narcissist may react with deep hostility. Narcissists rarely accept responsibility for the problems in the relationship, and they often blame their partner for any issues that arise. When a partner dares to assert themselves or challenge the narcissist's control, they may be met with rage, manipulation, or guilt-tripping. The narcissist sees any attempt to assert boundaries as a threat to their fragile sense of superiority, and they will punish their partner accordingly.

The Complexity of Narcissism

Recognizing a narcissist's true nature can be difficult, especially because they often present themselves as charming, confident, and even humble. This is particularly true for covert narcissists, who tend to fly under the radar by masking their grandiosity behind a guise of humility or quiet charm. This can make it difficult for friends and family to understand what's really going on in the relationship. From the outside, a narcissist might seem like a person of high status or someone worthy of admiration, but beneath the surface, their actions are often manipulative and self-serving.

A phenomenon known as trauma bonding can make it especially hard for victims to leave. Narcissists frequently use intermittent reinforcement, a cycle where they reward their partner with moments of affection, kindness, or validation, followed by periods of neglect or abuse. This creates a deep emotional attachment that makes the partner feel like they are addicted to the relationship. The highs and lows become a kind of emotional drug, and leaving feels nearly impossible, even if the partner recognizes the abusive behavior. It takes time, support, and emotional healing to break free from this cycle.

For many survivors, narcissistic abuse becomes a pattern of repetition in future relationships. Because narcissists often target individuals with high empathy or strong qualities, survivors may find themselves repeatedly drawn to partners who exhibit similar patterns of manipulation. This isn't about weakness; it's about unresolved trauma and patterns formed in childhood or past relationships. Helping survivors recognize these patterns is a crucial step in their healing journey.

The Aftermath of Narcissistic Breakups

Finally, the breakup with a narcissist is rarely a "normal" breakup. The narcissist will often continue the abuse or escalate it post-breakup. They may attempt to hoover their ex back into the relationship with love-bombing tactics, but if that doesn't work, they may resort to smear campaigns, threats, or stalking. This continuation of abuse after the relationship ends is one of the most distressing aspects of narcissistic abuse.

The discovery that a former partner has Narcissistic Personality Disorder (NPD) can be a shocking and traumatic realization. It often feels like mourning the death of a person you thought you knew. The illusion of the loving, caring partner you once believed in evaporates, and you are left to grapple with the painful truth that you were manipulated and abused.

Recognizing the Realities

Understanding these difficult truths about narcissistic abuse can help you better support survivors. It may be hard to accept the depths of manipulation and the lasting effects that narcissists have on their victims. But by acknowledging these realities, you can offer empathy, understanding, and validation to those who have suffered. Healing from narcissistic abuse is a journey, but it starts with recognizing the manipulative behaviors for what they truly are and offering a supportive, compassionate space for recovery.

CHAPTER TEN

SUPPORTING A SURVIVOR

"Sometimes, the best way to support a survivor is simply to listen without judgment and remind them they are not alone."

When a friend or family member opens up about experiencing narcissistic abuse, it can be a difficult and emotional moment. Narcissistic abuse is often hidden beneath a facade of charm and control, leaving the victim feeling isolated, confused, and powerless. The scars left by this kind of emotional manipulation can be deep and long-lasting. As someone who cares about the survivor, your support can make a world of difference in their healing process. Understanding the nature of narcissistic abuse and how to best provide support is crucial. This chapter outlines practical and compassionate ways to help someone who is recovering from the pain and trauma caused by a narcissist.

1. Believe Them: The Foundation of Support

Why Believing Matters

One of the most important ways to support someone who has experienced narcissistic abuse is simply to believe them. It may seem like an obvious starting point, but for a victim of narcissistic abuse, being believed can be one of the most powerful sources of validation. Narcissistic abuse often involves patterns of manipulation, gaslighting, and emotional control that can sound unbelievable to those who haven't witnessed them firsthand. Survivors may share stories of being publicly humiliated, being accused of things they didn't do, or having their perceptions constantly challenged. These behaviors can be hard to grasp for someone who has not experienced them, but it is vital to offer unconditional belief in their account.

Example

Imagine a friend tells you about how their boss routinely belittles them in front of colleagues but then denies any wrongdoing when confronted. To an outsider, this may sound extreme or exaggerated. However, the experience for your friend is real, and their pain is valid. Narcissistic bosses often use humiliation and gaslighting to maintain control over their subordinates. By believing them, you validate their feelings and help them feel less alone in their suffering.

How to Show Belief

Listen Actively: Offer your full attention when your friend speaks about their experience. Avoid interrupting or offering immediate solutions. Sometimes, the most healing thing you can do is to listen without judgment.

Avoid Judgment: Resist the urge to question their perceptions or say things like, "That doesn't sound possible" or "Maybe you misunderstood." Instead, show empathy by acknowledging the difficulty of their experience. For example, saying, "I can't imagine how painful that must have been" can go a long way in helping them feel heard.

2. Don't Minimize Their Experience

Understanding Minimization

A common response from friends and family, whether out of ignorance or a desire to offer reassurance, is to minimize the survivor's experience. Phrases like "Just get over it" or "It's not that bad" may seem harmless, but they can be deeply damaging. Narcissistic abuse is not just "a rough patch" or a temporary issue—it's a form of sustained emotional harm that can shake a person's sense of self-worth. Minimizing their experience can invalidate their feelings and make them feel as though their pain isn't important. This can also reinforce the shame they already feel, as narcissistic abusers often work to convince their victims that they are overreacting or imagining things.

Example

If a friend confides, "My partner is constantly belittling me, making me feel worthless," a response like "Well, everyone gets criticized sometimes" undermines the specific emotional abuse they are enduring. It might make them feel like their suffering is unimportant or even trivial, which can increase their sense of isolation.

How to Avoid Minimization

Acknowledge Their Pain: Validate their feelings and acknowledge that what they are going through is difficult. You might say, "What you're describing sounds really tough, and I'm so sorry that you've had to deal with that."

Offer Empathy Without Judgment: Allow them to express their feelings without offering immediate solutions or dismissing their experiences. Sometimes, just saying, "I believe you, and I'm here for you" can offer immense comfort.

3. Consider Your Relationship with the Abuser

The Impact of Your Relationship

When you know the abuser personally, it can create a delicate and challenging dynamic. If the abuser is someone within your social circle or family, maintaining a relationship with them may feel like a betrayal to the survivor. They may feel that you are condoning or overlooking the abusive behavior, especially if the abuser hasn't faced any real consequences for their actions. Survivors of narcissistic abuse often feel alone in their suffering, and if they believe that the people around them are still engaging with the abuser, it can exacerbate their sense of betrayal.

Example

If your friend's abusive ex is also a mutual acquaintance, continuing to socialize with this person might unintentionally signal to your friend that you don't take their pain seriously. They might feel unsupported or that you are aligning yourself with the person who caused them harm.

How to Navigate This

Evaluate Your Relationship: Reflect on whether maintaining a relationship with the abuser is necessary and how it affects your support for the survivor. While you don't necessarily have to cut ties with the abuser, it's important to consider the impact that ongoing contact may have on the person you're trying to support.

Communicate Transparently: If you decide to continue a relationship with the abuser, be honest with the survivor about your decision. Reassure them that your support remains unwavering and that you are committed to standing by them. This transparency helps prevent misunderstandings and strengthens your bond with the survivor.

4. Educate Yourself

The Importance of Education

One of the most powerful tools you can arm yourself with when supporting a survivor of narcissistic abuse is knowledge. Narcissistic abuse often involves emotional manipulation, gaslighting, and psychological control, which can be difficult to recognize and understand if you haven't seen it firsthand. Victims of narcissistic abuse are often made to feel crazy, unworthy, or overly sensitive, so understanding the dynamics of this type of abuse can help you offer more effective support. By educating yourself, you'll be better equipped to offer empathy and advice that is grounded in an understanding of the specific trauma they have endured.

Example

A survivor may describe how their partner uses the silent treatment as a form of control, leaving them feeling invisible and unimportant. While this may seem like a minor issue, it is a form of psychological abuse that can deeply affect someone's mental health. Recognizing the harmful effects of emotional manipulation can help you respond with more compassion and insight.

How to Educate Yourself

Read and Research: There are countless books, articles, and online resources available that explore the dynamics of narcissistic abuse. Start with credible sources to understand how narcissists manipulate and control their victims. Books like "The Sociopath Next Door" by Martha Stout or "Psychopath Free" by Jackson MacKenzie can provide valuable insights.

Attend Workshops and Support Groups: Support groups for survivors of narcissistic abuse can be incredibly helpful in learning how to best support your loved one. These groups provide a safe space for sharing experiences and advice and often offer resources on coping strategies.

5. Be Patient and Compassionate

Understanding the Recovery Process

Healing from narcissistic abuse is not a linear process. Survivors may experience periods of intense pain, confusion, and self-doubt. They might struggle with feelings of guilt, shame, or fear of being judged. Additionally, many survivors have a hard time recognizing their own worth after being systematically devalued by a narcissistic abuser. Recovery can take time, and your role is not to rush the process but to offer a consistent, compassionate presence.

Example

Your friend might go through phases where they question whether the abuse was truly as bad as they remember, or they might go back to the abuser out of fear or confusion. These are common signs of trauma bonding, and while frustrating, it's important to remain patient and supportive, rather than pushing them to "move on" or "snap out of it."

How to Be Patient

Avoid Pressuring Them: Let them move at their own pace. If they are not ready to take certain steps—whether it's leaving the abuser or confronting the trauma—be understanding. Pressuring them could create further feelings of inadequacy.

Offer Consistent Support: Let them know you are there for them no matter what. Small gestures of care, like checking in, offering to spend time together, or just being present, can make a big difference.

Empowering the Survivor:

Supporting a friend or family member who has endured narcissistic abuse can be emotionally challenging, but it is also one of the most important things you can do for them. By believing their experiences, avoiding minimization, considering your relationship with the abuser, educating yourself about narcissistic behavior, and practicing patience and empathy, you can be a vital source of healing and strength. It's crucial to remember that recovery is a process, and your unwavering support can help them rebuild their sense of self-worth, regain their confidence, and ultimately break free from the trauma of narcissistic abuse. With time, compassion, and understanding, survivors can heal—and your role as a supportive ally will be a powerful part of their journey.

CHAPTER ELEVEN

LIFE AFTER THIS EXPERIENCE

"Life after trauma is not about forgetting the past; it's about embracing the strength you've gained and moving forward with purpose."

Ending a significant relationship—especially one with a narcissist—can feel like stepping into a storm. The whirlwind of emotions that follows is overwhelming, disorienting, and often full of contradictions. Whether you made the decision to leave for your own well-being or the relationship ended because of circumstances beyond your control, the aftermath can be just as tumultuous as the relationship itself. However, this journey through emotional chaos isn't just a painful process of grief and loss. It's also a period of self-discovery, healing, and growth. Although it may feel impossible at times, there is hope on the other side. The key is to embrace the emotional landscape that comes with ending a toxic relationship and trust that, with time, you will find peace and reclaim your sense of self.

Navigating the Emotional Landscape

The period after cutting contact with a narcissist is one of intense emotional turmoil. The pain doesn't just vanish because the relationship is over—if anything, it intensifies. The absence of the narcissist can feel like a vast, empty space. It's not just the loss of a person but the loss of a world you once knew, a world that was dominated by their presence and their control. In the early days, it's easy to feel disoriented, unsure of who you are or where you fit in without them. The challenge is to embrace this difficult emotional terrain and allow yourself to feel every emotion that arises—whether it's anger, sadness, regret, or confusion. Each feeling is a part of the healing process.

Example:

Imagine waking up to an empty house, with no one beside you in the bed where they once slept. The absence feels palpable, almost suffocating. Routines that once felt comforting—like making breakfast together or having late-night conversations—now seem unfamiliar, leaving you to face the silence. What once felt like a shared life now feels like a void. This loss, though painful, is the first step toward healing, and though it feels vast and unfillable in the moment, it will begin to shift over time.

The Struggle of Letting Go

Letting go after a relationship with a narcissist is not as simple as severing ties. It is not just about walking away physically but also emotionally. The relationship has likely been a rollercoaster of highs and lows, making it difficult to leave behind the moments of affection or idealization. Narcissistic abuse often works in cycles—periods of charm followed by periods of devaluation, leaving you attached to the highs. This attachment can make the process of letting go more complicated. The desire to return, to fix things, to recapture the good moments can be overwhelming. You may find yourself obsessing over old memories or scrolling through their social media, hoping for some sign that they miss you or that they have changed.

Example:

You catch yourself late at night scrolling through old photos of happy times, moments when you thought everything was fine. You long for the warmth of their embrace, the laughter you shared, and the illusions of a perfect future you once imagined. But deep down, you know those moments were fleeting, and the relationship was built on manipulation and control. The urge to reach out to them for "closure" can be intense. However, breaking the no-contact rule often only prolongs the pain. The closure you seek doesn't lie in another conversation with them but in finding it within yourself.

Embracing the Healing Process

Healing is not linear, and there is no one-size-fits-all timeline. After leaving a narcissistic relationship, healing requires deep introspection and a willingness to face the emotions you might have avoided for so long. During this time, it's important to recognize that healing is a process that will take time. Every emotion you feel—whether it's anger, sadness, regret, or guilt—is valid, and it's essential not to rush through them. Instead of suppressing your feelings, let them come and go as they need to. The more you allow yourself to feel, the faster you can move through the stages of grief and begin to heal.

Example:

One day, you may be able to get out of bed and do something as simple as go for a walk. That might feel like a major accomplishment after the emotional weight of the previous days. Each small victory in the healing process is significant. Perhaps you try a new hobby or reconnect with friends you may have neglected during the relationship. The key is to be patient and gentle with yourself, acknowledging every step you take, no matter how small.

During this time, you may also come to some painful realizations about yourself and the relationship. It's common to recognize that you may have lost yourself in the relationship—prioritizing their needs over your own or sacrificing your values and boundaries to keep the peace. These insights, though hard to digest, are crucial for your personal growth. Understanding how you got caught in these patterns can help you break free from them in future relationships.

Example:

You might come to realize that you neglected your own emotional needs to please your ex. You might have ignored red flags or excused their behavior because you wanted to believe in the idealized version of them that they showed you at the beginning. Acknowledging this pattern is painful but necessary. It allows you to take back control of your life and rebuild your self-esteem and sense of identity.

Moving Forward and Finding Peace

As you heal, it's important to recognize that you won't be the same person you were before the relationship. While the pain of the past may always be a part of you, it doesn't define who you are or your future. The goal isn't to forget what happened, but to learn from it and use those lessons to create a healthier, happier future for yourself. Missing the narcissist, even after all they've put you through, is natural. After all, love—no matter how toxic—can leave deep emotional scars. But it's important to remind yourself that missing them doesn't mean you should return to the relationship.

Example:

Imagine learning that your ex has already moved on with someone else. A wave of hurt and jealousy washes over you, and for a moment, it stings. But then you remind yourself that their journey is theirs alone, and your healing is what matters most. The end of the relationship doesn't signal the end of your life—it signifies the beginning of a new chapter. The journey ahead is yours to shape, and the only way forward is through the lessons you've learned.

The Journey Ahead

The road after leaving a narcissistic relationship may seem long, winding, and filled with uncertainty, but it also holds the potential for profound personal growth and transformation. Over time, the sharp edges of your emotions will begin to soften, and you will find your footing again. Healing doesn't happen overnight, and there will be moments of doubt and pain along the way, but the key is to keep moving forward. The end of the relationship might have closed one door, but it opens others—doors that lead to your own empowerment and peace.

Example:

A year from now, you might look back on this chapter of your life and feel a deep sense of pride in how far you've come. You've learned about your own strength, gained resilience, and discovered that your worth was never defined by someone else's ability to love or respect you. You've learned that self-love and personal boundaries are essential to healthy relationships. Most importantly, you've learned that you deserve happiness, peace, and respect. The road ahead is full of possibilities, and each step forward is a step toward a more fulfilling, authentic life.

Embracing Life After Narcissistic Abuse

Life after narcissistic abuse is challenging, but it is also filled with possibility. You are no longer defined by the relationship or the abuse you endured. You are not the sum of your past experiences but the sum of how you choose to rise from them. The pain you feel now will eventually transform into strength and wisdom. Your worth was never tied to their treatment of you, and as you reclaim your life, you will learn to value yourself in ways that will guide you into healthier, more loving relationships—both with others and with yourself.

Trust the process. Embrace the journey. And know that every step you take forward is a step toward a brighter, more peaceful future.

CHAPTER TWELVE

STABLE WELLNESS

"Stable wellness is the harmony of mind, body, and spirit, allowing you to thrive even in the face of life's challenges."

Welcome to the final stage of your recovery journey! If you've made it here, you've already fought through the most intense phases of healing. This chapter marks a critical milestone—the point where your emotional and mental wellness begins to stabilize, where the progress you've made can start to feel more permanent. You've climbed a difficult mountain, and though you may still encounter challenges ahead, the summit is now within sight. Take a moment to breathe in the fresh air, appreciate the view, and reflect on how far you've come. This stage is about solidifying your hard-earned peace and ensuring that it becomes your new way of living, where you actively protect the progress you've made.

Celebrating Your Strength

At this point in your recovery, it's vital to take stock of just how much strength you've demonstrated. Healing from narcissistic abuse is not easy, and the fact that you've made it this far is a testament to your resilience. For so long, your sense of self-worth may have been compromised, and your emotional well-being may have been in constant turmoil. Now, you've managed to find stability, and you've learned that your peace is something worth protecting.

A profound quote encapsulates this stage beautifully: "When we know how to be happy, we won't tolerate being around someone who makes us unhappy." This statement highlights a pivotal realization. You've learned how to prioritize your well-being, and you now recognize that it is non-negotiable. You've developed a deeper understanding of what makes you feel secure, healthy, and at peace, and you're not willing to compromise on that again.

However, as you embrace this newfound peace, you might notice that others perceive you differently. Some may view you as overly guarded or too selective about the people you let into your life. While their judgments may sting, it's important to remember that protecting your emotional boundaries is a form of self-care, not isolation. Not everyone deserves access to the healthier, stronger version of you that you've worked so hard to build.

Example:

Think of it this way—if you've just finished an intense workout routine and your muscles are sore and tender, you wouldn't let anyone push on them or put pressure on them. You'd protect them, allow them time to heal, and be mindful of any unnecessary strain. In the same way, your emotional wellness is a muscle that you've spent time strengthening and restoring. Now that it's in a more stable place, it's crucial to protect it from any future emotional strain or harm.

Protecting Your Healing

Your healing process is a precious, fragile thing, and protecting it should be a top priority. This stage of your journey isn't just about keeping distance from the person who abused you—whether through No Contact or Detached Contact—but also about preventing any future emotional damage. The healing you've cultivated requires ongoing effort and attention. While life may inevitably throw curveballs, and challenges may arise, you now have the tools to face them without reopening old wounds or inviting the toxic behaviors you've worked so hard to leave behind.

It's common for survivors of narcissistic abuse to feel hesitant when it comes to new relationships, whether romantic or platonic. While it's natural to want connection, it's also essential to be discerning. Don't feel guilty about taking the time you need to evaluate who you allow into your life. Trust your instincts and remain vigilant about setting boundaries. The goal is not to live in fear but to recognize when someone's behavior might resemble the manipulative tactics of your past abuser.

Example:

Suppose you meet a new colleague who is charming, confident, and seemingly kind. Initially, you might feel a sense of relief, thinking that you can finally interact with someone who isn't toxic. But over time, you notice that they begin to make subtle criticisms, manipulate situations to make themselves appear more favorable, or dismiss your feelings when you try to express concerns. In this case, your past experiences have equipped you with the skills to recognize red flags before they escalate. Rather than letting them back into your life, you can set a clear boundary and protect yourself from the potential harm.

Avoiding Old Patterns

One of the most challenging aspects of this phase of recovery is resisting the temptation to slip back into old patterns of behavior. After enduring narcissistic abuse, it's easy to romanticize the fleeting positive moments of the past—those moments when the narcissist charmed you, validated your worth, or appeared to love you in their own distorted way. It's essential to stay grounded and remind yourself of the reality of the relationship.

For those of you in Detached Contact—where you maintain limited communication or are keeping boundaries but not fully cutting ties—it's crucial to remember that toxic people rarely change. Narcissists may offer small bursts of kindness or charm, but they are often temporary and manipulative. Don't allow the fleeting good moments to cloud your judgment or cause you to compromise the progress you've made.

For those in No Contact, this stage can feel particularly liberating, but it's essential to stay vigilant against falling into old relational patterns. It might be tempting to reach out to your former abuser for "closure" or to seek validation. But remember that closure is something you provide for yourself. You don't need them to give you permission to move on. Your healing comes from inside you, not from anything they could offer.

Example:

It's like looking at an old picture of a vacation where everything seemed perfect at the time. When you reflect on the moment, you might recall the happiness, the fun, or the beautiful surroundings. But if you allow yourself to remember the full context—the fights, the emotional manipulation, the lies—you can put that moment into perspective. It wasn't perfect, and it wasn't healthy. Allow yourself to see the entire picture and avoid falling into the trap of romanticizing the past.

Embracing Transformation

This stage of recovery is where transformation truly begins to unfold. You are no longer the person you were when you entered the relationship or even when you started the healing process. Through all the challenges, you've emerged stronger, wiser, and more self-aware. Your relationship with yourself has shifted, and you now recognize your own worth and capacity for happiness. Embrace this transformation and let it empower you to seek out healthier connections.

As you embrace this new chapter, you'll find that your expectations for relationships have evolved. No longer will you tolerate toxic behaviors or compromise your values for the sake of someone else. Instead, you'll seek out relationships that are built on respect, mutual support, and genuine love.

Example:

Think about buying new clothes after losing weight or transforming your physical health. Initially, you might find yourself reaching for the same size or style of clothing you wore before, even though your body has changed. It takes some time to realize that your new body requires a new wardrobe. Similarly, as you heal from narcissistic abuse, you'll find that you no longer fit into the old relational patterns or toxic dynamics from your past. Embrace the changes, and be open to the healthier connections that await you.

Reflecting on Your Goals

As you settle into this new chapter of your life, take some time to reflect on what you truly want from the future. Ask yourself: What does a high-quality life look like for me? Write down your goals and values, and reflect on what you've already achieved. What do you still want to accomplish? What are the core values that will guide your choices moving forward?

This isn't just about relationships—this is about creating the life you've always wanted, independent of anyone else's expectations. Whether your goals involve personal growth, achieving financial stability, pursuing your passions, or building self-love, take this time to think about what truly matters to you. Break free from the patterns of the past and allow your vision for the future to guide you.

Example:

Perhaps you've always wanted to travel but put it on hold because of the narcissistic partner who discouraged your dreams. Now that you've freed yourself from their control, you can start planning your adventures, not just for the sake of escaping but for the joy of discovering new places and experiences. Similarly, maybe you've always wanted to pursue a career change or start your own business. Now is the time to take bold steps toward those goals and build a future on your own terms.

Moving Forward

As you continue your healing journey, it's important to remember that this is not the end. Life is a continuous journey of growth, and it's okay to revisit this book or any resources that help guide you on your path. Each time you read through your journey, you'll find new insights, new ways to nurture your healing, and new opportunities to apply what you've learned. Remember, the abuse was never your fault. It's your time now to apply your newfound wisdom and live a life that reflects your true worth.

Keep Dreaming

The future is full of possibilities. You've already shown yourself how strong, capable, and worthy you are of love, respect, and happiness. Now, it's time to embrace the future with open arms. Keep dreaming, keep growing, and trust that you are deserving of a life filled with love, peace, and fulfillment. The best is yet to come.

This is your time. Keep moving forward with confidence. You've earned it.

CHAPTER THIRTEEN

Choosing Your Response: Mindful Reactions

"How we respond shapes our reality; by embracing mindfulness and choosing kindness, we empower ourselves to rise above negativity and nurture our own peace."

Understanding narcissism is a pivotal step, but how we respond to these behaviors can make all the difference in maintaining our own peace and kindness. In this chapter, we'll explore the importance of mindful reactions and practical strategies for choosing responses that protect our well-being while promoting a positive environment.

The Power of Mindfulness

Mindfulness is the practice of being fully present and aware of our thoughts, feelings, and surroundings without judgment. When interacting with a narcissistic individual, mindfulness can help us remain calm and centered, allowing us to choose our reactions rather than defaulting to emotional responses.

Pause Before Reacting: When faced with a provocation, take a moment to breathe deeply and assess your feelings. This brief pause can prevent you from reacting impulsively and allow for a more measured response.

Acknowledge Your Emotions: It's normal to feel anger, frustration, or sadness when dealing with narcissistic behavior. Acknowledge these emotions without letting them control you. Journaling or talking to a trusted friend can help you process these feelings.

Reframe Your Perspective: Try to view the situation through a different lens. Recognizing that the narcissist's behavior stems from their own insecurities can help you respond with compassion rather than anger.

Choosing Constructive Responses

Once you're in a mindful state, you can choose how to respond in a way that aligns with your values and promotes kindness:

Use "I" Statements: Instead of pointing fingers or assigning blame, express how you feel using "I" statements. For example, "I feel overwhelmed when the conversation turns negative" can foster more constructive dialogue.

Stay Calm and Collected: Maintain a calm demeanor, even when the other person is not. Your composed presence can diffuse tension and set a positive tone for the interaction.

Set Clear Boundaries: If the conversation becomes toxic, don't hesitate to assertively set boundaries. You can say something like, "I'm not comfortable discussing this right now," which protects your peace without escalating conflict.

Focus on Solutions: Redirect the conversation toward problem-solving rather than dwelling on negativity. This shift not only keeps the interaction productive but also reinforces your commitment to a positive mindset.

Practicing Self-Care

Engaging with narcissistic individuals can be draining. Prioritize self-care to recharge and maintain your kindness:

Engage in Activities You Enjoy: Make time for hobbies and activities that bring you joy and relaxation, whether it's reading, exercising, or spending time with loved ones.

Practice Gratitude: Reflect on the positive aspects of your life. Keeping a gratitude journal can help you focus on what truly matters and counterbalance negative experiences.

Seek Support: Surround yourself with a supportive network that uplifts you. Sharing your feelings with friends or a therapist can provide perspective and encouragement.

Choosing how to respond to narcissistic behavior is not always easy, but with practice, it becomes more natural. By incorporating mindfulness and constructive communication strategies into your interactions, you can foster an environment of kindness and respect. Ultimately, these choices empower you to remain true to your values and create a more positive life for yourself, regardless of the challenges you face.

As you continue on this journey, remember that your reactions define your experience. Embrace the power of mindful responses, and watch how it transforms your interactions and your overall outlook on life.

Redefining Your Values

"By redefining our values and living with intention, we reclaim our power; in prioritizing kindness and resilience, we create a life that truly reflects our authentic selves."

In the journey of healing from relationships marked by narcissism or abuse, one of the most transformative steps is redefining your values. Often, those who seek to manipulate or control may attempt to isolate you from your core beliefs and values, leaving you feeling lost and disconnected. This chapter focuses on how to intentionally shift your lifestyle to prioritize kindness, resilience, and personal growth, helping you reclaim your sense of self.

Recognizing the Impact of Isolation

Abusers often thrive on isolating their victims, creating an environment where their values overshadow those of the individual. This isolation can lead to:

Confusion: Being constantly exposed to someone else's distorted reality can make you question your beliefs.

Self-Doubt: When your values are undermined, it's easy to lose confidence in your decisions and identity.

Fear of Rejection: You may feel that embracing your true values could lead to further isolation or conflict.

Recognizing these effects is the first step in reclaiming your power. Understand that your values are not only valid; they are essential to your well-being.

Identifying Your Core Values

To redefine your values, start by identifying what truly matters to you. Take time to reflect on the principles that resonate with your authentic self:

Self-Reflection: Set aside quiet time to journal or meditate on your values. What do you believe in? What principles guide your actions?

Create a Values List: Write down a list of core values—such as kindness, honesty, resilience, compassion, and growth. This visual reminder can serve as a touchstone during difficult moments.

Assess Alignment: Consider how your current lifestyle aligns with these values. Are there areas where you feel you're compromising your beliefs for the sake of maintaining peace or avoiding conflict?

Living with Intention

Once you have identified your core values, the next step is to consciously integrate them into your daily life:

Set Intentional Goals: Create specific, actionable goals that align with your values. For example, if kindness is a core value, set a goal to perform one act of kindness each day.

Mindful Decision-Making: Before making decisions, ask yourself how they align with your values. This practice can help you stay grounded and focused on what truly matters.

Cultivate Resilience: Embrace challenges as opportunities for growth. Resilience allows you to bounce back from setbacks and stay true to your values even when faced with adversity.

Surround Yourself with Support: Build relationships with individuals who share your values and uplift you. Positive connections reinforce your commitment to living intentionally and can provide strength during challenging times.

Embracing Kindness and Compassion

Prioritizing kindness—both towards yourself and others—can be a powerful antidote to the negativity you may have experienced. Here's how to embrace kindness as a core value:

Practice Self-Kindness: Treat yourself with the same compassion you would offer a friend. Acknowledge your feelings, celebrate your achievements, and forgive your mistakes.

Engage in Acts of Kindness: Small acts, whether offering support to a friend or volunteering, can reinforce your commitment to kindness and create positive ripples in your community.

Reflect on Impact: Consider how your actions affect others. When you prioritize kindness, you not only enhance your own life but also contribute to a more compassionate world.

Staying Focused Amid Distractions

As you redefine your values and strive to live intentionally, remember that the journey may not always be easy. Distractions and negativity can arise, especially from those who wish to undermine your growth. Here are some strategies to stay focused:

Regular Check-Ins: Schedule regular check-ins with yourself to assess how well you're aligning with your values. Adjust your goals and actions as needed.

Create Affirmations: Develop positive affirmations that reinforce your commitment to your values. Repeat these affirmations daily to strengthen your resolve.

Seek Guidance: If you find it challenging to stay focused, consider seeking guidance from a mentor, therapist, or support group. They can provide encouragement and accountability.

Redefining your values is a powerful act of self-empowerment. By prioritizing kindness, resilience, and personal growth, you create a life that reflects your authentic self. Remember that you are not defined by the actions of others; you have the strength to rise above and live with intention.

As you navigate this journey, hold fast to your values, knowing that they are the compass guiding you toward a brighter, more fulfilling future. Embrace the beauty of living intentionally, and watch how it transforms not only your life but also the lives of those around you.

CHAPTER FIFTEEN

FREEING YOURSELF FROM RESENTMENT

"Forgiveness is a gift we give ourselves; by letting go of resentment, we open our hearts to healing, joy, and new beginnings."

Forgiveness is often misunderstood. It's not about condoning harmful behavior or forgetting the past; rather, it's a powerful act of self-liberation. This chapter will explore the importance of embracing forgiveness as a means to free yourself from resentment and reclaim your emotional well-being.

Understanding Forgiveness

Forgiveness begins with recognizing that holding onto resentment serves no purpose other than to weigh you down. It can cloud your judgment, drain your energy, and prevent you from moving forward. By understanding what forgiveness truly means, you can start to release its misconceptions:

Forgiveness is Personal: It's a gift you give to yourself, not to the person who hurt you. It allows you to let go of the burden of anger and hurt.

It's a Process: Forgiveness isn't instantaneous; it's a journey that requires time and effort. Allow yourself to feel the emotions that arise without judgment.

Forgiveness Doesn't Equal Reconciliation: You can forgive someone without needing to restore the relationship. Setting boundaries can be an important part of this process.

The Impact of Resentment

Resentment is like a poison that can seep into every aspect of your life, affecting your mental, emotional, and even physical health. When you harbor resentment, you may experience:

Emotional Turmoil: Constantly reliving the hurt can lead to anxiety, sadness, or anger, making it difficult to enjoy life.

Impaired Relationships: Resentment can create walls between you and those you care about, hindering connections and intimacy.

Stagnation: Holding onto the past can keep you from pursuing new opportunities or experiences, trapping you in a cycle of negativity.

The Path to Forgiveness

Embracing forgiveness requires intentionality and self-reflection. Here are steps to guide you on this journey:

Acknowledge Your Feelings: Allow yourself to feel the hurt, anger, or betrayal. Acknowledgment is the first step toward healing. Journaling can be an effective tool for processing these emotions.

Understand the Impact: Reflect on how holding onto resentment affects your life. Consider the weight it carries and the way it shapes your thoughts and actions.

Shift Your Perspective: Try to view the situation from a different angle. Consider the other person's experiences and motivations. This doesn't excuse their behavior but can help you cultivate empathy.

Make a Conscious Choice: Decide that you want to forgive. This commitment is a powerful step toward freeing yourself from resentment.

Express Forgiveness: You might choose to express forgiveness directly to the person or do so privately through a letter you don't send. The act of articulating your feelings can be liberating.

Focus on the Future: Redirect your energy toward personal growth and future possibilities. Create goals that align with your values and aspirations, reinforcing a sense of purpose.

The Healing Power of Forgiveness

As you embrace forgiveness, you'll likely notice profound changes in your emotional landscape:

Inner Peace: Letting go of resentment opens the door to a greater sense of calm and tranquility, allowing you to live in the present.

Improved Relationships: Releasing past grievances can create space for healthier, more meaningful connections with others.

Renewed Energy: Freed from the burden of resentment, you'll find renewed energy and enthusiasm for life. This vitality can inspire you to pursue new opportunities and experiences.

Enhanced Resilience: Forgiveness builds emotional resilience, enabling you to navigate future challenges with a clearer mind and an open heart.

Embracing forgiveness is a courageous journey toward liberation. By freeing yourself from resentment, you reclaim your power and open yourself to a brighter future. Remember, forgiveness is not about the other person; it's about your healing and growth.

As you move forward, carry with you the understanding that forgiveness is an ongoing practice. It may take time and effort, but with each step, you draw closer to a life defined by peace, authenticity, and joy. Embrace this journey, and watch how it transforms your life from within.

CHAPTER SIXTEEN

LIVING YOUR TRUTH

"Living your truth means choosing authenticity over approval; it's the fearless act of honoring who you are, unbound by the opinions of others."

In a world filled with noise and expectation, living authentically can feel like an act of rebellion. Many of us have been conditioned to seek validation from others, measuring our worth by their opinions. But what if the greatest freedom comes from embracing who we truly are, regardless of external approval?

The Cost of Seeking Approval

When we chase approval over authenticity, we risk losing sight of ourselves. We might find ourselves mired in self-doubt, constantly comparing our lives to others, or conforming to what we think people want us to be. This relentless pursuit can drain our energy and leave us feeling disconnected from our true selves.

Embracing Your Authentic Self

To reclaim your authenticity, start by embarking on a journey of self-discovery. Dive deep into your passions, values, and beliefs. What makes your heart race? What principles do you want to guide your life? Creating a list of core values can help clarify your identity, reminding you of what truly matters. Embracing your authentic self means accepting imperfections and recognizing that nobody is flawless. Celebrate your unique qualities—those quirks and idiosyncrasies that make you, well, you. Cultivating self-compassion is crucial; it's about treating yourself with the same kindness you'd offer a dear friend.

Accepting Others' Perspectives

As you begin to live authentically, you may notice that not everyone understands your journey. Some people might doubt your experiences or question your choices. This can be disheartening, but accepting that their perspectives are limited can be liberating. It's a reminder that their inability to comprehend your truth doesn't diminish its validity. In these moments, choose to be the bigger person. Instead of reacting defensively, embrace compassion for their misunderstanding. Everyone is navigating their own challenges, often unseen.

Choosing Authenticity Over Approval

Letting go of the need for approval isn't always easy, but it can be transformative. Mindfully consider your decisions: are they aligned with your true self, or are they made out of a desire for acceptance? Celebrate your uniqueness and find strength in what sets you apart. Instead of striving for perfection, focus on being real. Self-expression is a powerful way to affirm your authenticity. Whether through art, writing, or simply sharing your thoughts, allow yourself to speak your truth without fear of judgment. It's in this vulnerability that we often connect most deeply with others.

The Rewards of Living Authentically

Living authentically brings a multitude of rewards. As you align your life with your true self, you'll likely find a boost in confidence. Authenticity fosters genuine relationships; when you're true to yourself, you attract people who appreciate you for who you really are. This creates deeper, more meaningful connections. Moreover, authenticity cultivates resilience. When grounded in your true self, you can navigate challenges with greater clarity and courage. Life becomes a journey filled with purpose, rooted in the joy of pursuing what matters most to you.

Ultimately, living your truth is a brave and empowering act. It requires commitment, but the freedom it brings is worth every effort. Your worth is not dictated by others; it lies within your unique existence. Embrace your individuality and allow yourself to be vulnerable. As you navigate this path, remember that it's okay if not everyone understands your experience. The true measure of growth lies in your ability to rise above external judgments and remain anchored in who you are. In doing so, you'll create a life that radiates purpose, connection, and joy—a life that celebrates the essence of you.

UNDERSTANDING THE UNFORTUNATE

"To understand the unfortunate is to recognize that beneath their actions lies a deeper pain; compassion allows us to heal while holding firm to our own values."

When confronted with the pain inflicted by a narcissist or abuser, it's easy to view them as an enemy. Their actions can feel hurtful and dehumanizing, leading to anger and resentment. However, shifting our perspective can be a powerful tool in our healing journey. Instead of seeing them as adversaries, we can recognize them as individuals grappling with their own internal battles. This chapter explores how to maintain your values while fostering a compassionate outlook toward those who hurt you.

Reframing the Narrative

Understanding narcissism as a mental health issue rather than a personal attack can help you reframe your experiences. Narcissists often exhibit behaviors rooted in deep-seated insecurities and unresolved trauma. By viewing them through this lens, you can begin to see their actions as symptoms of their struggles, not as direct assaults on your character.

Recognizing Their Pain: Individuals with narcissistic traits often carry wounds from their past. Their behavior may stem from a desire to protect themselves from vulnerability, leading to destructive patterns. Acknowledging this can help you approach the situation with empathy rather than hostility.

Choosing Compassion Over Anger: Compassion doesn't mean excusing harmful behavior; rather, it means understanding the motivations behind it. By choosing to view the narcissist as an unfortunate person rather than a foe, you protect your emotional wellbeing from the corrosive effects of anger.

Protecting Your Values and Emotions

While it's important to cultivate compassion, it's equally vital to establish boundaries that safeguard your values and emotional health. Here's how to balance compassion with self-protection:

Set Clear Boundaries: Establishing boundaries is essential when dealing with narcissistic individuals. Protect your time, energy, and emotional space. Communicate your limits clearly and stick to them. This not only safeguards your wellbeing but also sends a message about what you will and will not accept.

Prioritize Your Wellbeing: Make self-care a priority. Engage in activities that nourish your spirit and strengthen your resilience. Surround yourself with supportive people who respect your boundaries and encourage your growth.

Practice Emotional Detachment: Learn to detach emotionally from the narcissist's behavior. Their reactions are often reflections of their inner turmoil and not a commentary on your worth. By reframing their actions as projections of their struggles, you can protect your emotions from unnecessary hurt.

Supporting Them, When Appropriate

In certain situations, you may feel inclined to support a narcissistic individual towards stability, but this must be approached carefully:

Offer Help Wisely: If the opportunity arises to support them in a constructive manner, do so cautiously. Encourage them to seek professional help if they are open to it. Suggesting therapy or counseling can provide them with tools to address their issues, but remember that change must come from within.

Avoid Enabling Behavior: While compassion is important, avoid falling into patterns of enabling. Supporting someone doesn't mean allowing their harmful behaviors to continue unchecked. Stay firm in your boundaries, even as you offer understanding.

Be Realistic: Understand that change takes time, and not everyone is ready to confront their issues. While you can offer support, you are not responsible for their healing. Protect your own journey first.

Finding Strength in Compassion

Approaching a narcissist with compassion doesn't negate your pain; rather, it empowers you to rise above it. By recognizing them as individuals facing their own challenges, you free yourself from the cycle of resentment and anger.

Cultivate Empathy: Empathy can be a transformative practice. By understanding their struggles, you cultivate a sense of peace within yourself. This doesn't mean you condone their actions, but it allows you to navigate the relationship with a clearer mind.

Embrace Your Growth: As you practice compassion, celebrate your growth. You're choosing to respond to pain with understanding rather than retaliation, which is a powerful testament to your character.

Foster Inner Peace: Compassion for others, combined with strong personal boundaries, creates a harmonious balance. You can support someone's journey without compromising your own values, leading to a more peaceful existence.

Viewing a narcissist or abuser through the lens of compassion allows you to reclaim your power while maintaining your values. This approach isn't about excusing harmful behavior, but rather recognizing the complexities of human experience.

By protecting your emotional health and boundaries, you can navigate these challenging relationships without losing sight of who you are. Embrace the strength that comes from compassion, and let it guide you toward a more peaceful, authentic life—one where you honor both your journey and the human struggles of others. In this way, you cultivate a resilience that can withstand even the toughest challenges, emerging stronger and more self-aware.

CHAPTER EIGHTEEN

BEING A BEACON OF KINDNESS

"From the ashes of trauma, let your kindness be the spark
that inspires change; by sharing your light, you guide
others toward healing and hope."

Emerging from the shadows of narcissistic abuse is not just a personal victory; it's a transformative journey that can light the way for others. When you rise from pain and reclaim your strength, you become a beacon of kindness, capable of inspiring change and fostering a community rooted in compassion. This chapter is about harnessing your experiences to spark positive change and inspire kindness in the lives of those around you.

The Power of Personal Experience

Your journey through suffering is filled with lessons that can resonate deeply with others. Each challenge faced and each insight gained creates a powerful narrative that others can draw upon for strength. Sharing your story is not just about recounting pain; it's about illuminating a path for those who feel lost.

Sharing Your Truth: When you speak openly about your experiences, you validate the struggles of others who may feel isolated in their pain. Your truth can connect hearts, reminding others that they are not alone on their journey.

Cultivating Empathy: Having walked through the fire, your capacity for empathy has likely deepened. This newfound understanding allows you to relate to others in profound ways, inspiring them to extend kindness in their own lives.

Demonstrating Resilience: Your story of overcoming adversity is a powerful testament to resilience. By showcasing your triumphs, you motivate others to confront their own challenges with renewed courage.

The Ripple Effect of Kindness

Kindness is a potent force, capable of creating ripples that extend far beyond your immediate circle. When you embody kindness, you inspire those around you to do the same, fostering an environment where compassion flourishes.

Modeling Kindness: Your actions can set off a chain reaction. Simple acts of kindness—like offering a listening ear or a warm smile—can inspire those around you to respond in kind, creating a culture of care.

Encouraging Others: Invite friends and family to engage in acts of kindness, whether through volunteering or random acts of compassion. This collective effort can transform a community, making kindness the norm rather than the exception.

Creating Safe Spaces: Foster environments where people feel comfortable expressing their feelings and vulnerabilities. By encouraging open dialogue, you nurture connection and understanding, paving the way for deeper relationships.

Turning Pain into Purpose

Your suffering can become a powerful catalyst for change. As you heal, consider how you can turn your pain into purpose, helping others navigate their own paths.

Volunteering and Advocacy: Get involved in community service or support organizations that focus on mental health and awareness of abuse. Your involvement amplifies your voice and creates essential resources for those in need.

Starting Conversations: Use your experiences to spark important discussions about narcissistic abuse and its effects. Opening up these conversations can destigmatize the struggles many face, fostering greater understanding in society.

Writing and Sharing: Consider writing articles, starting a blog, or even speaking publicly about your journey. Your words can reach those who feel unheard, providing them with hope and guidance.

The Transformative Power of Kindness

As you inspire others to embrace kindness, remember that true change begins within. Cultivating kindness in your own heart empowers you to influence those around you.

Practice Self-Compassion: Before extending kindness to others, make sure you're kind to yourself. Acknowledge your journey and celebrate your growth; self-compassion is the bedrock for sharing kindness outwardly.

Be Mindful: Practicing mindfulness helps you stay present and aware in your interactions. This awareness allows you to respond to others with empathy and kindness, even in challenging situations.

Nurture Positive Relationships: Surround yourself with individuals who uplift and inspire you. Building a supportive network amplifies the impact of your kindness and creates a nurturing environment for all.

Inspiring change through kindness is not just an act; it's a legacy you have the power to create. Your journey from suffering to healing equips you with the wisdom to uplift others. As you shine your light, you become a beacon of hope for those still in the shadows.

Remember that every act of kindness, no matter how small, contributes to a larger movement of compassion. By sharing your story, modeling kindness, and fostering understanding, you help cultivate a world where empathy triumphs over indifference. Together, we can transform our suffering into a powerful force for good, inspiring kindness and connection in every corner of our lives. Through your experiences, you can ignite change, turning pain into purpose and creating a brighter future for all.

CHAPTER NINETEEN

Bhagavad Gita on Narcissistic Karma

The Bhagavad Gita offers profound insights into the nature of human action (karma), the ego, and spiritual growth. For survivors of narcissistic abuse, these teachings offer a powerful way to understand the karmic consequences of narcissism and to embark on a journey of healing. By exploring the Gita's wisdom on karma, the ego, and divine qualities, we can break free from toxic patterns, reclaim our peace, and heal from the damage caused by narcissistic abuse.

Karma: The Law of Cause and Effect

The concept of karma—the law of cause and effect—is central to the Gita. Every action, thought, or intention we create has consequences, both immediate and long-term. In the case of narcissistic behavior, the narcissist's manipulative, exploitative actions—driven by pride, anger, and self-centeredness—set into motion a cycle of karmic repercussions. These actions affect not only the victim but ultimately the abuser as well, even if they are unaware of it.

Sloka 3.16 (Chapter 3 – Karma Yoga)

"Evam pravartitam chakram nanaanarthaa vidhiyate,
Aakratam karmano anyasya sadhasat abhivartate."

("Thus, the wheel of creation moves in a cycle, where actions—good or bad—will inevitably produce their results.")

In this verse, Krishna emphasizes the inevitable consequences of actions. Narcissists may seem to go unpunished in the short term, but every ego-driven action they take creates karmic consequences that will eventually catch up with them. The cycle of abuse continues until balance is restored through the law of karma.

For the survivor, understanding karma can be empowering. The narcissist's actions will return to them in time, but the focus should be on your own actions and healing. You are not bound to the abuser's destructive karma, but rather, you have the power to create positive karma by focusing on your healing journey.

The Nature of the Ego: Overcoming Narcissism

The ego is a central theme in the Gita, where it is called Ahamkara, or the false self. The ego is driven by pride, attachment, and the desire for control. Narcissism, at its core, is an exaggerated attachment to the ego—an inflated sense of self that overrides empathy for others.

Krishna teaches that the ego creates suffering, both for the individual and for those around them. The more attached one is to the ego, the more one is enslaved by it. Narcissists, driven by their ego, believe they are superior to others, entitled to special treatment, and deserving of control over others.

Sloka 3.27 (Chapter 3 – Karma Yoga)

"The person who acts with a sense of egoism, thinking 'I am the doer,' is deluded. The true self is detached from the actions of the body."

This verse highlights the delusion of the ego: the narcissist believes they are the center of the universe, unaware that their actions are ultimately driven by their false sense of self. The Gita teaches that true freedom comes when we detach from the ego and reconnect with our true nature, which is peaceful and selfless.

For the survivor, this means detaching from the narcissist's control and understanding that their behavior is driven by ego, not by true love or care. Healing begins when we stop reacting to the narcissist's manipulation and instead reconnect with our true self, which is beyond the reach of ego-driven behavior.

Cultivating Divine Qualities for Healing

In contrast to the narcissist's ego-driven behavior, the Gita teaches that cultivating divine qualities—humility, patience, forgiveness, and self-control—leads to spiritual growth and healing. These qualities are essential for overcoming the harm caused by narcissistic abuse.

Sloka 16.3 (Chapter 16 – Daivasura Sampad Vibhaga Yoga)

"Tejahkshamaa dhritir dakshyam yasho dyutam darpanam,
Satyam hridimahamschaiva daivi sampadamashritah."
("Fortitude, forgiveness, control over desires, and humility—these are the divine qualities that lead one toward liberation.")

The divine qualities Krishna speaks of are in stark contrast to the destructive traits of the narcissist, such as arrogance, pride, and cruelty. By embodying these qualities, survivors of narcissistic abuse can break free from the cycle of manipulation and reclaim their peace.

Fortitude: The strength to endure hardship without losing hope. Narcissistic abuse can be deeply painful, but fortitude enables us to move through the pain and continue on the path to healing.

Forgiveness: While forgiveness may seem difficult after experiencing narcissistic abuse, it is essential for freeing ourselves from the emotional hold of the abuser. The Gita teaches that forgiveness is not for the abuser, but for our own liberation.

Humility: Narcissistic abuse can leave one feeling small and unworthy. The Gita teaches that true humility comes from recognizing our inherent worth, independent of the validation or abuse from others.

Self-Control: Narcissists often provoke reactions to maintain control. Cultivating self-control allows us to disengage from the narcissist's emotional manipulation and preserve our inner peace.

By focusing on these divine qualities, we can begin to heal, rise above the narcissist's influence, and move toward spiritual growth.

Detachment: Freedom from the Narcissist's Grip

A key teaching of the Gita is the practice of detachment—not detaching from life itself, but from the fruits of our actions and the need for validation from external sources. This is especially important when dealing with narcissistic abuse, where emotional entanglement and a need for approval can keep the victim trapped in the cycle of manipulation.

Sloka 2.47 (Chapter 2 – Sankhya Yoga)

"Your right is to perform your duty only, but never to its fruits. Let not the fruits of action be your motive, nor let your attachment be to inaction."

In this verse, Krishna advises us to act without attachment to the outcome. For survivors of narcissistic abuse, this means letting go of the desire to change the narcissist or seek validation from them. Your focus should be on your own healing and growth, not on the narcissist's behavior.

Detachment allows us to stop reacting emotionally to the narcissist's provocations. It means recognizing that their actions are driven by their ego and their karma, and we are not bound to them. By focusing on your own journey and creating positive karma through self-care and healing, you free yourself from the narcissist's grip.

The Bhagavad Gita offers timeless wisdom for overcoming narcissistic abuse. By understanding the law of karma, the nature of the ego, and the importance of cultivating divine qualities like humility, forgiveness, and fortitude, we can break free from the cycle of suffering and begin the journey of healing.

The narcissist's karma is theirs to face, but our focus must be on our own actions—our healing, our self-care, and our spiritual growth. The Gita teaches that true freedom comes when we detach from the ego, whether our own or others', and reconnect with our true self, which is beyond the reach of manipulation and control.

By following the Gita's guidance, we can move from a place of suffering and fear to one of empowerment, peace, and spiritual growth. The key to healing lies in focusing on our own positive karma, cultivating divine qualities, and ultimately realizing our true nature as beings of light, compassion, and strength.